BLACK HISTORY LEGENDS

Copyright © 2020 by Graphikal Zen

All rights reserved. This book or any portion thereof
may not be reproduced or used in any manner whatsoever
without the express written permission of the publisher
except for the use of brief quotations in a book review.

Printed in the United States of America

9798604943373

BLACK HISTORY LEGENDS

BARACK OBAMA
The 44th president of the United States, and the first African American to serve in the office.

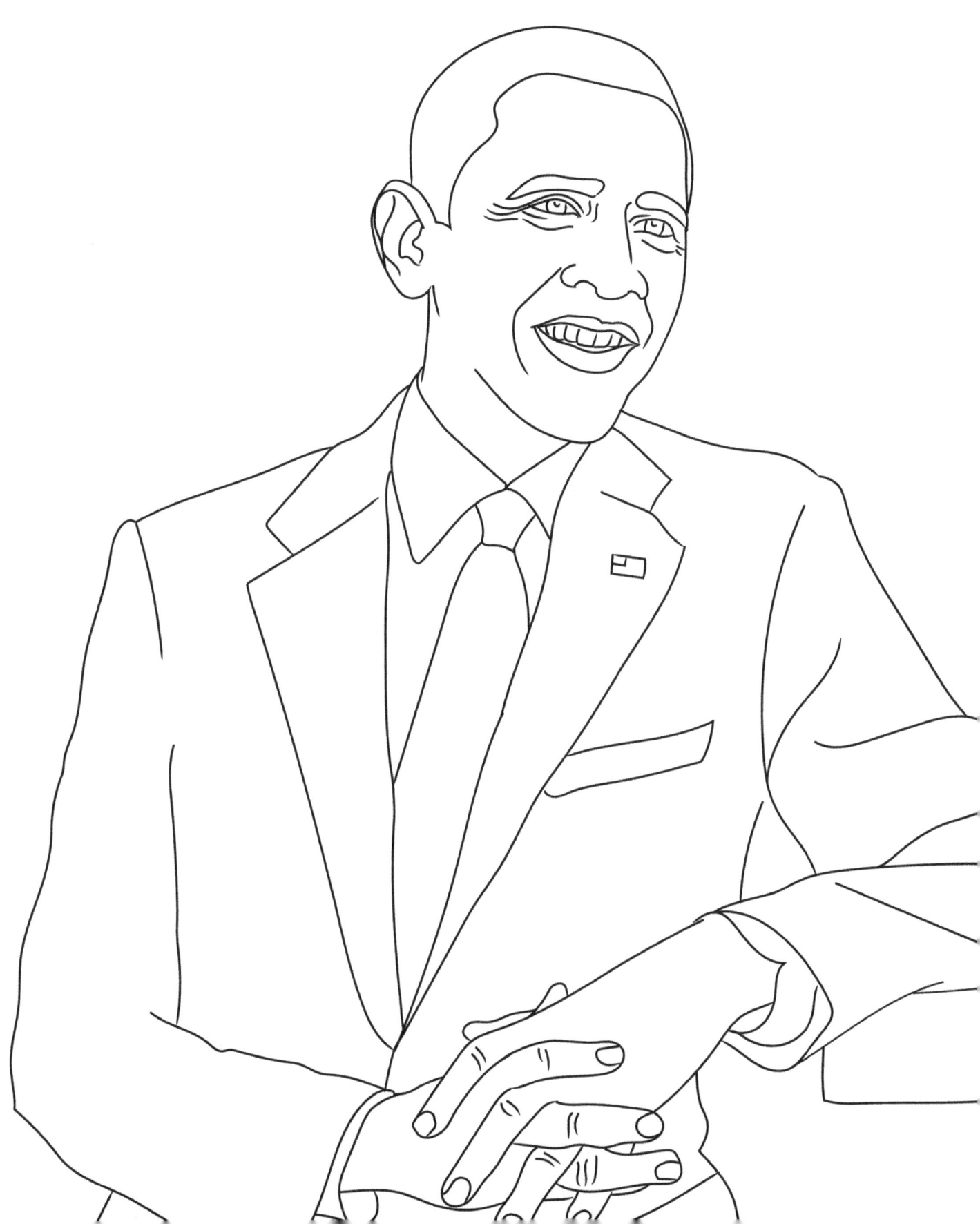

MICHELLE OBAMA
Lawyer, writer and wife of former U.S. President, Barack Obama.

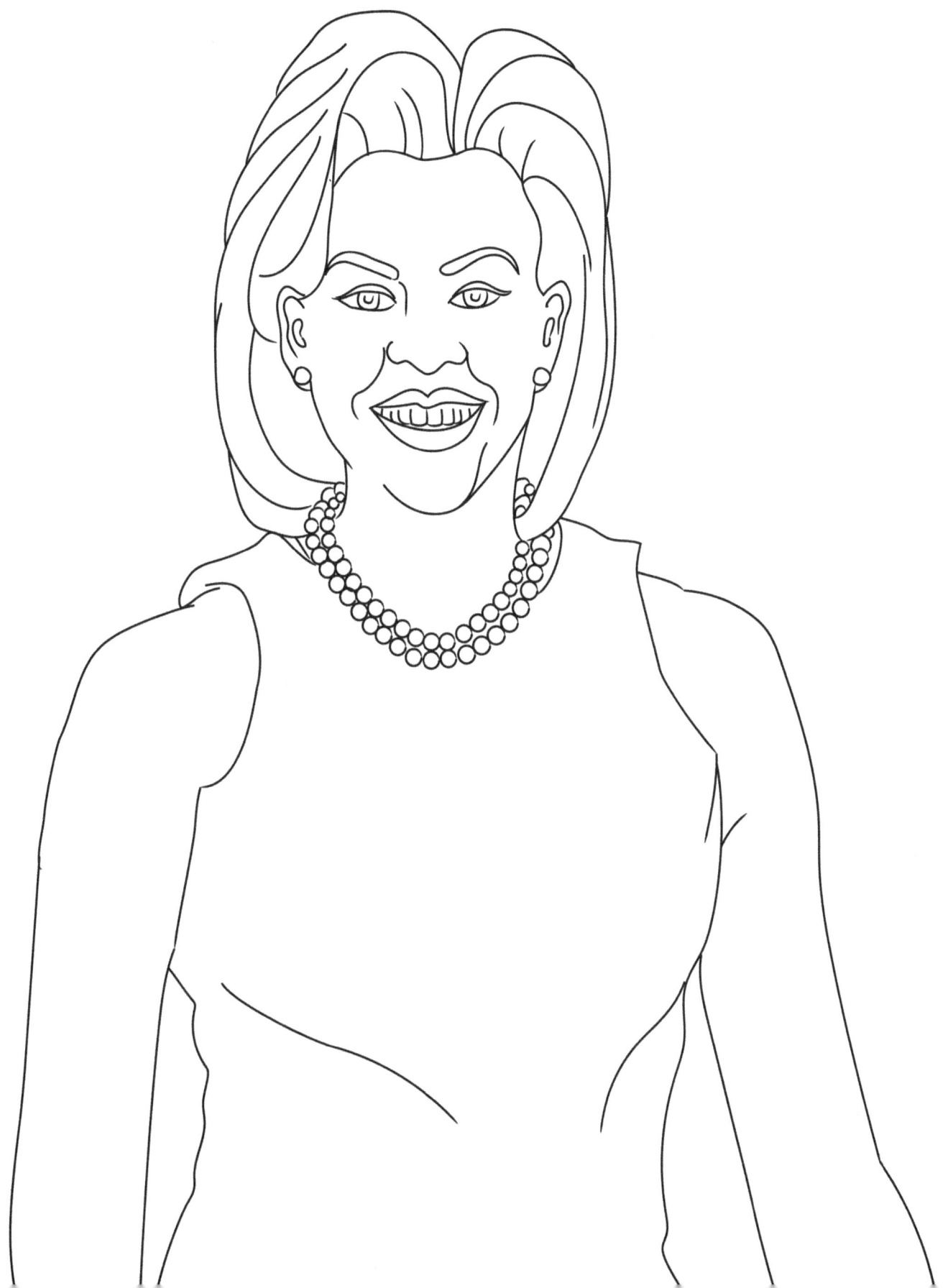

BLACK HISTORY LEGENDS

MAE JEMISON
First black woman to travel into space.

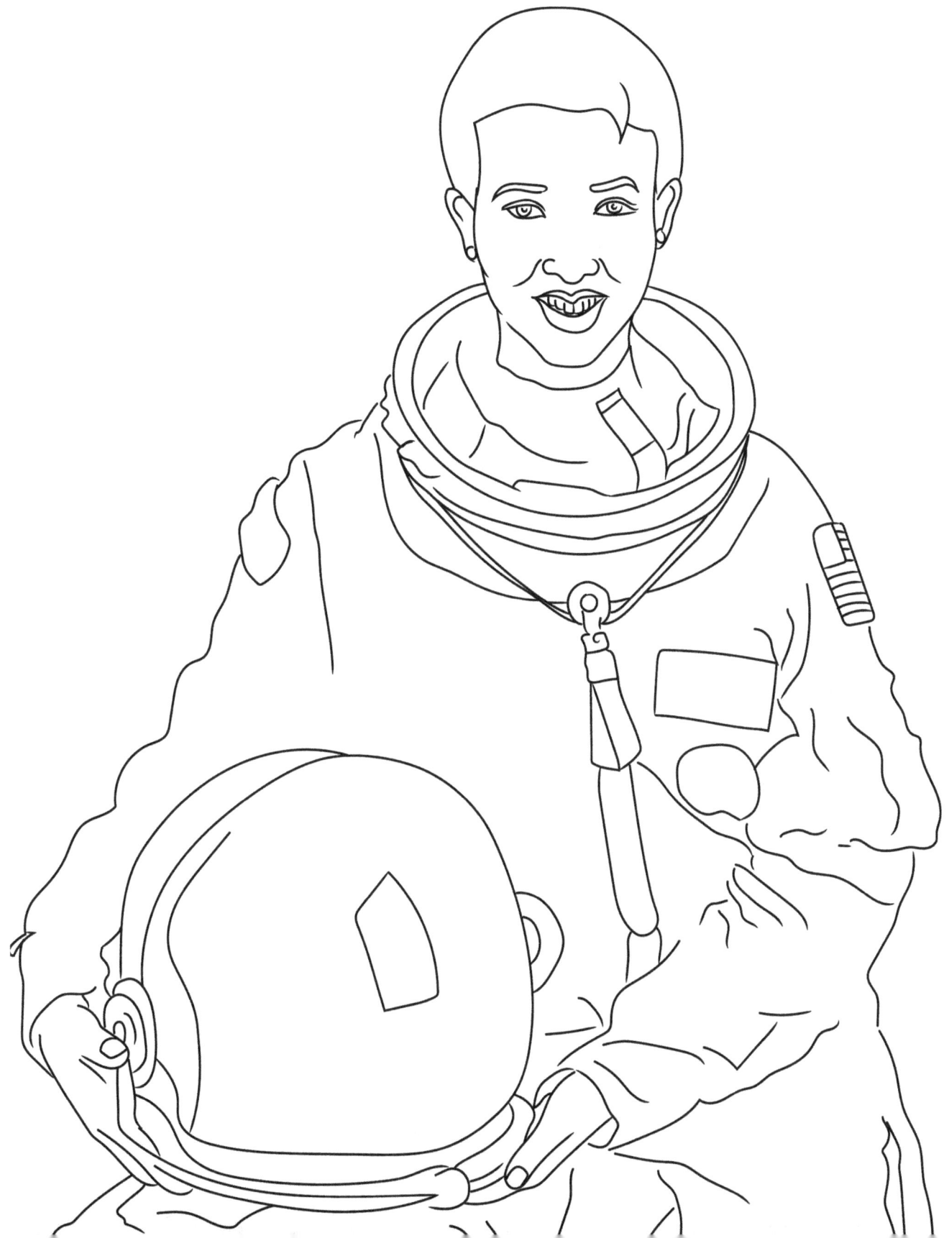

BLACK HISTORY LEGENDS

MARTIN LUTHER KING JR
Activist, scholar, and Civil Rights pioneer

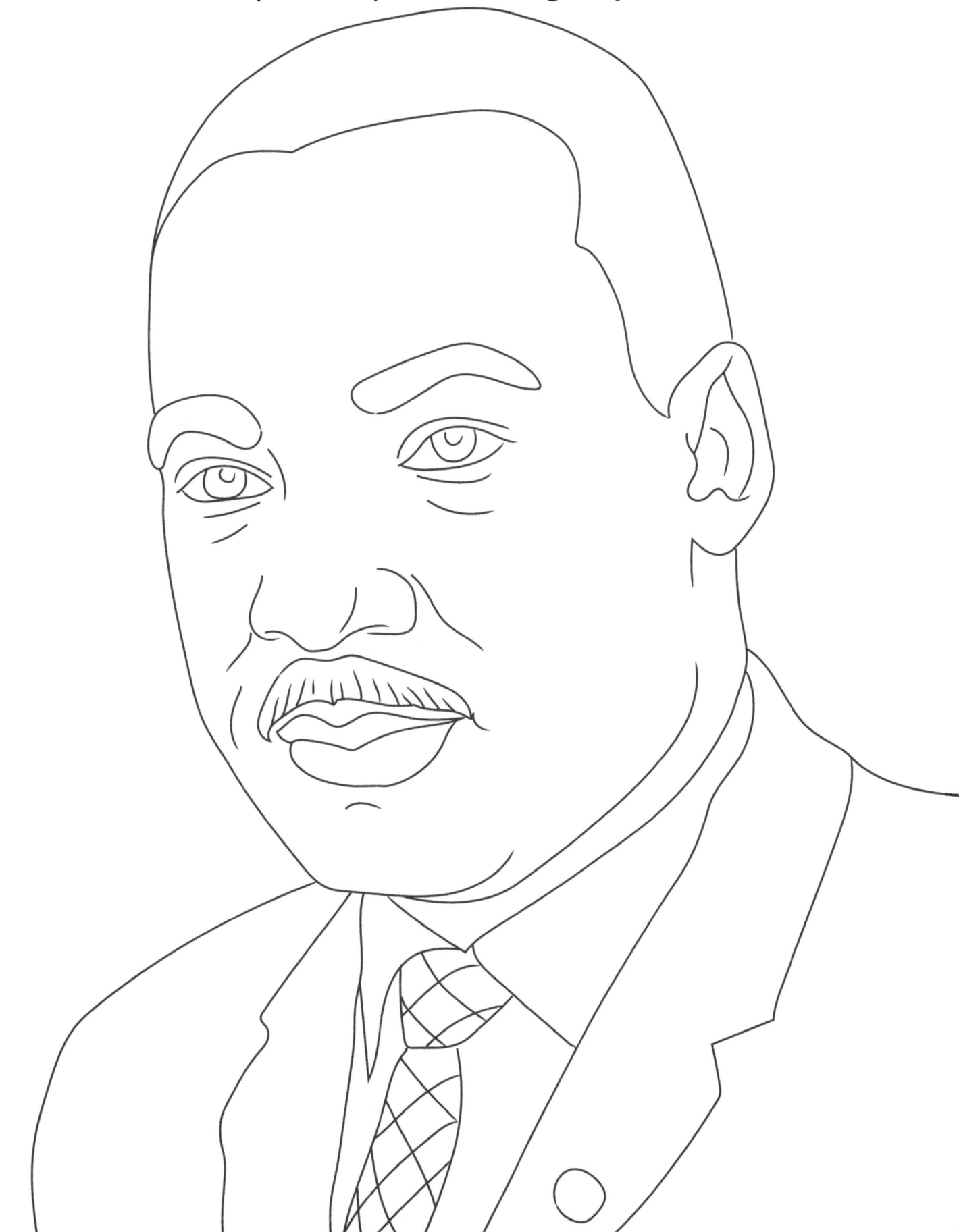

BLACK HISTORY LEGENDS

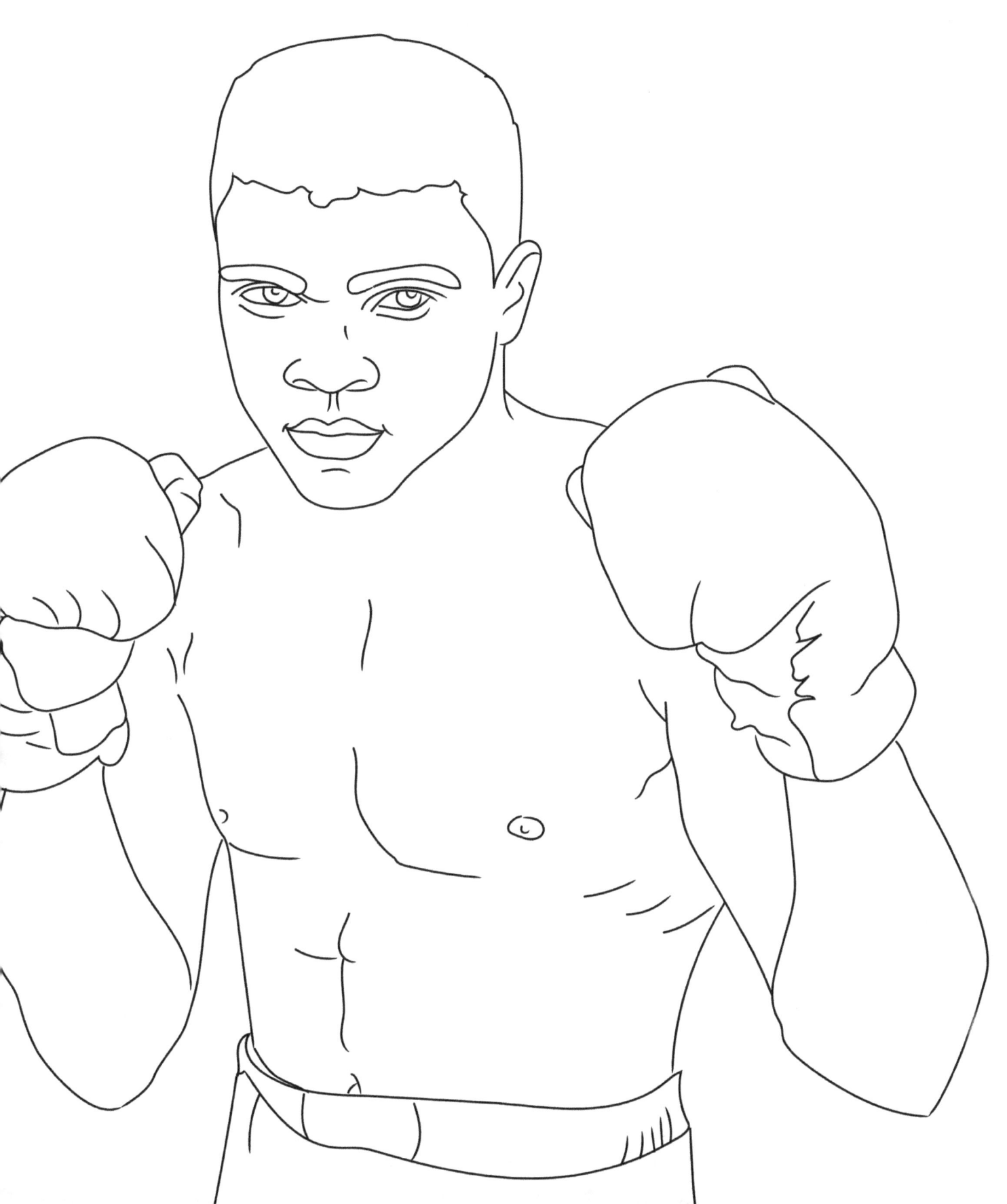

BLACK HISTORY LEGENDS

B.B. KING
Legendary musician regarded as the "King of Blues."

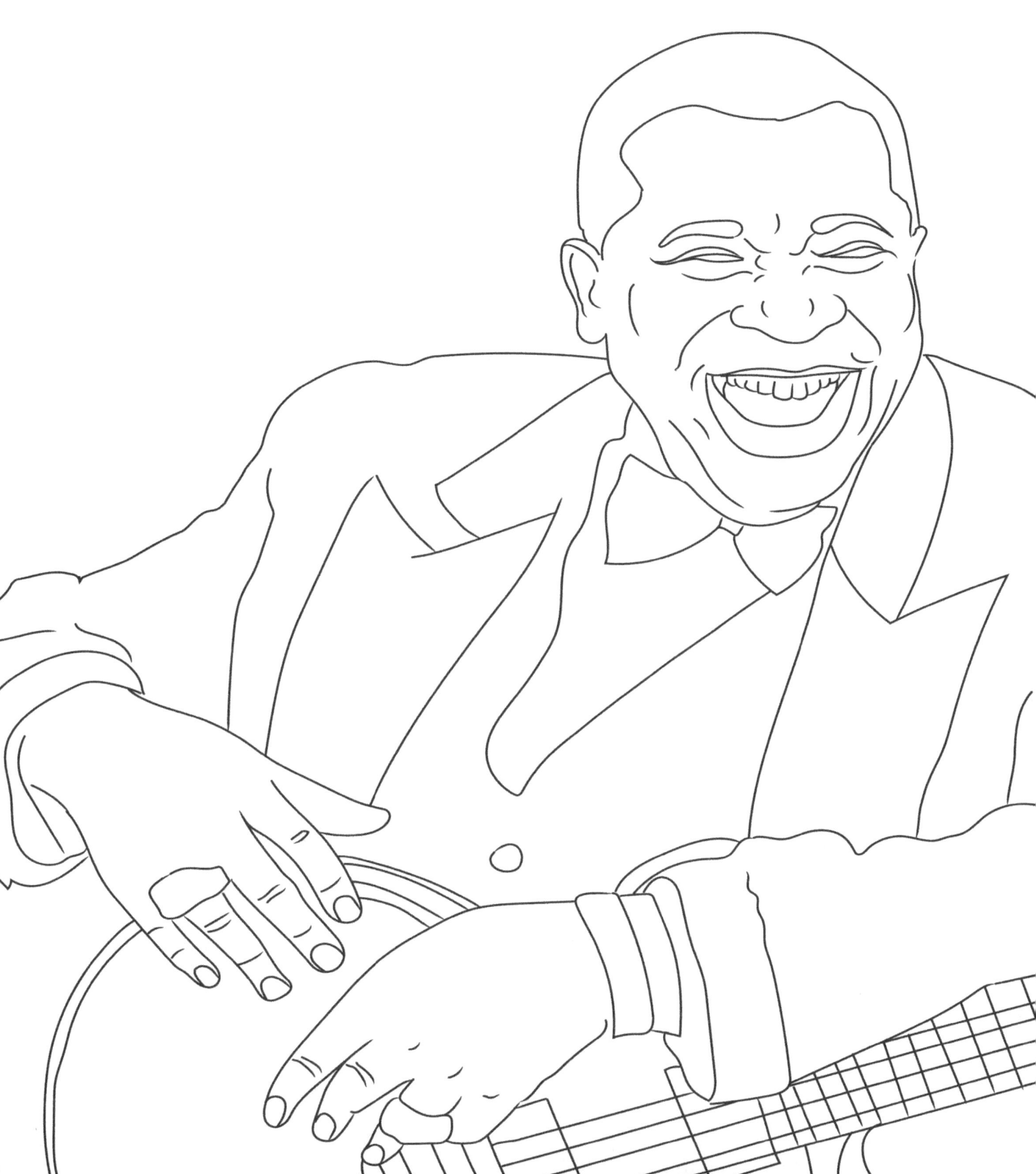

BLACK HISTORY LEGENDS

MALCOM X
Civil Rights leader and minister.

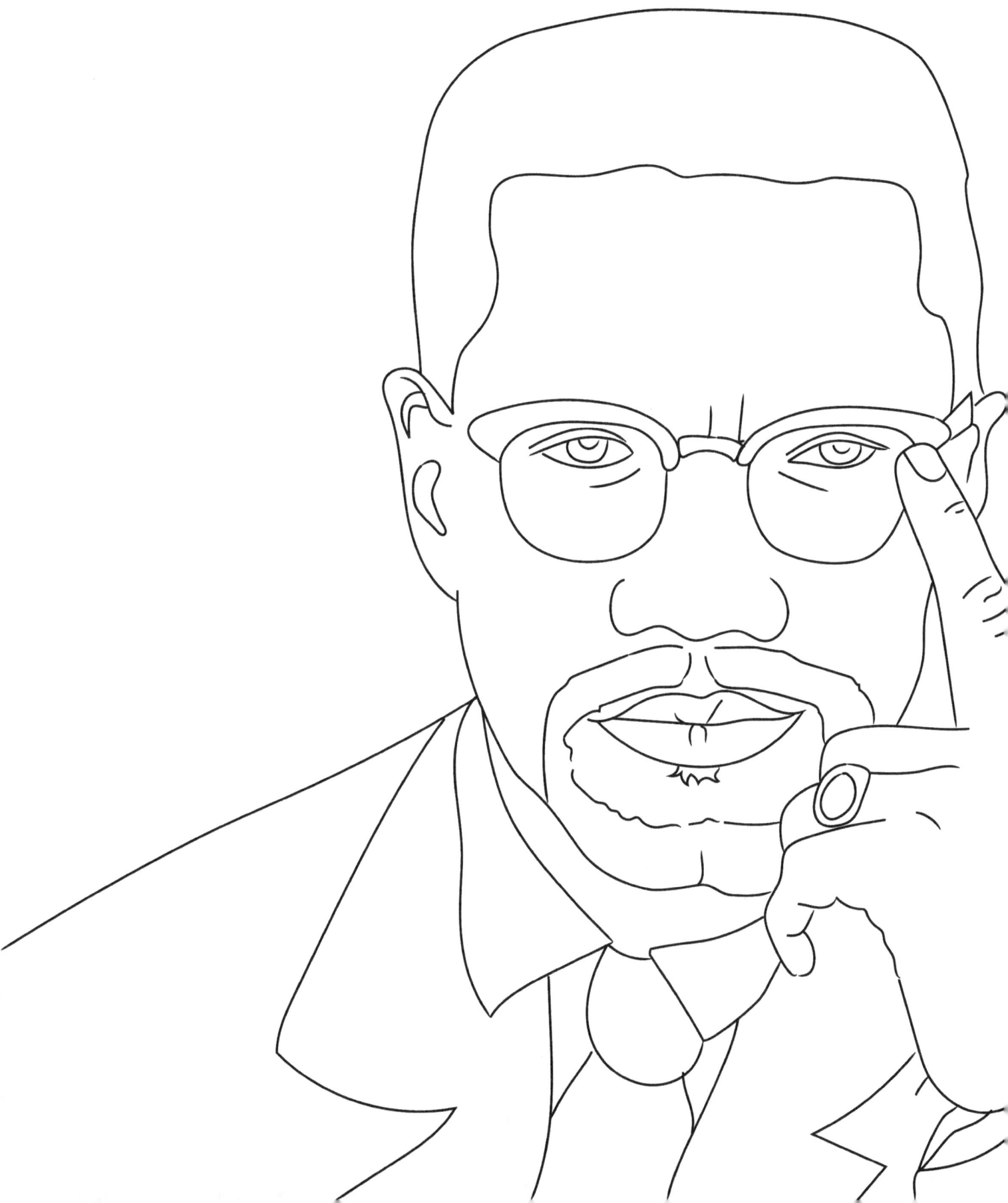

BLACK HISTORY LEGENDS

HARRIET TUBMAN

Abolitionist who led hundreds of slaves to freedom using the Underground Railroad.

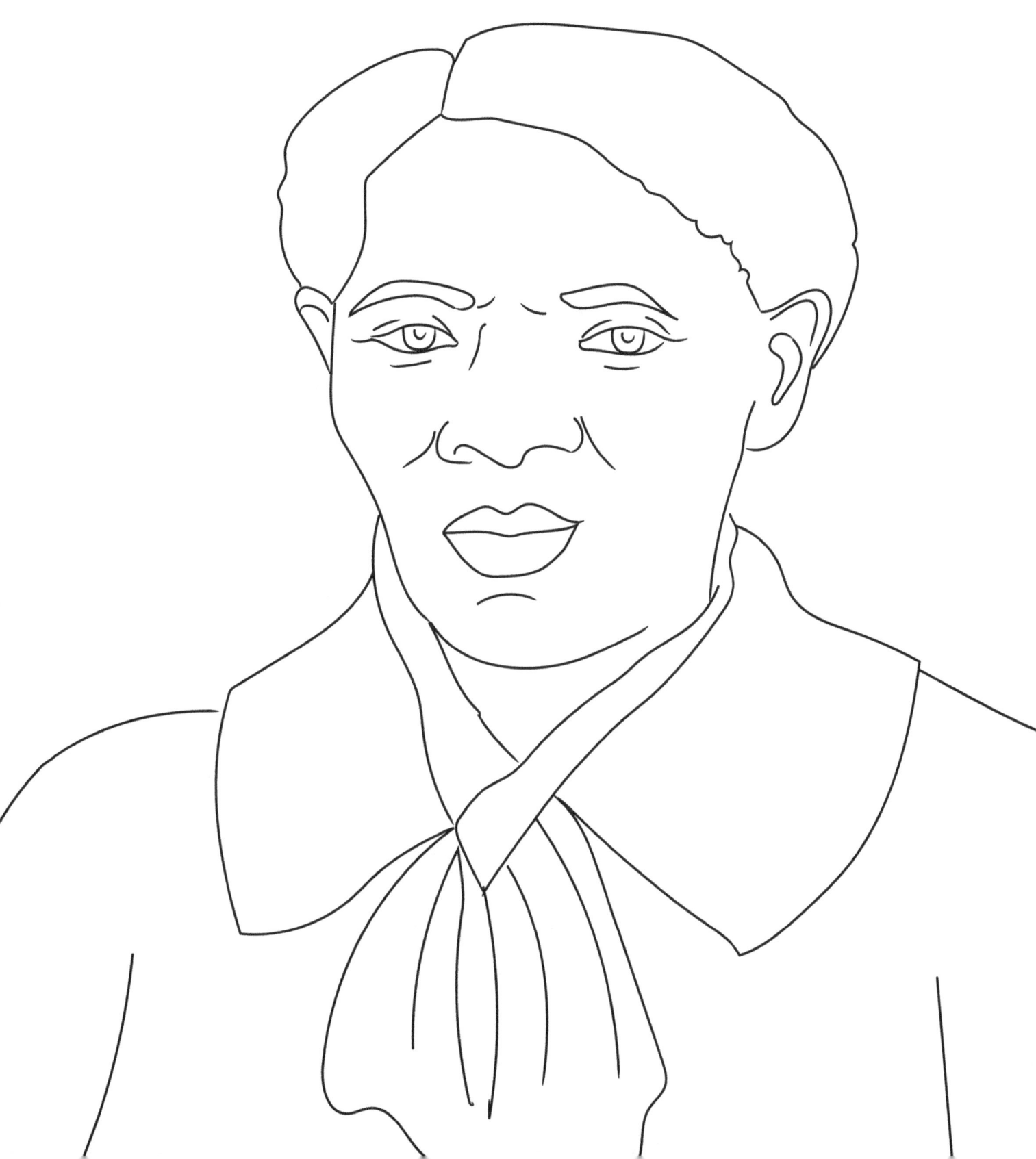

BLACK HISTORY LEGENDS

NINA SIMONE
Singer, songwriter, and civil rights activist.

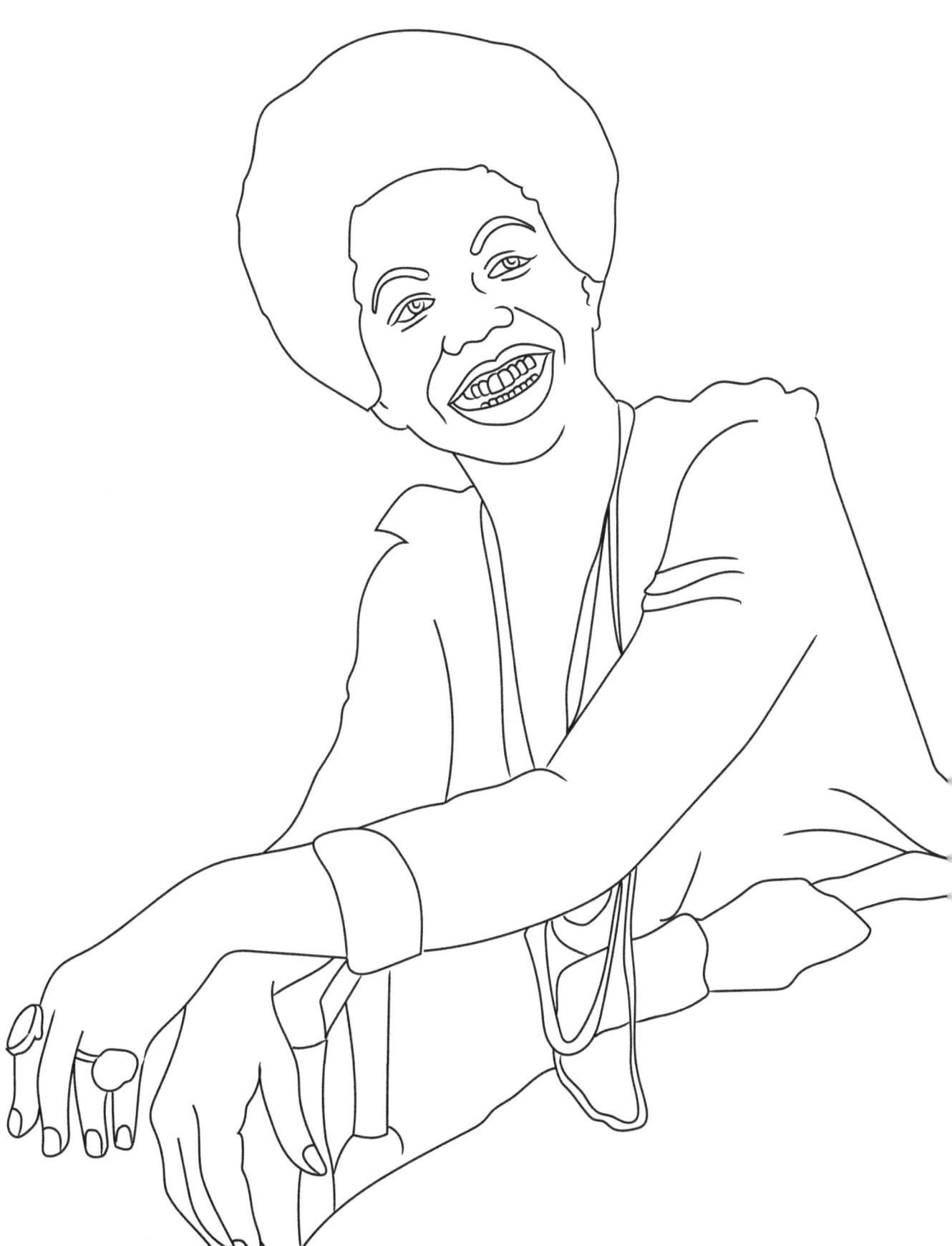

BLACK HISTORY LEGENDS

FREDERICK DOUGLASS

Escaped from slavery and eventually became a leader of the abolitionist movement.

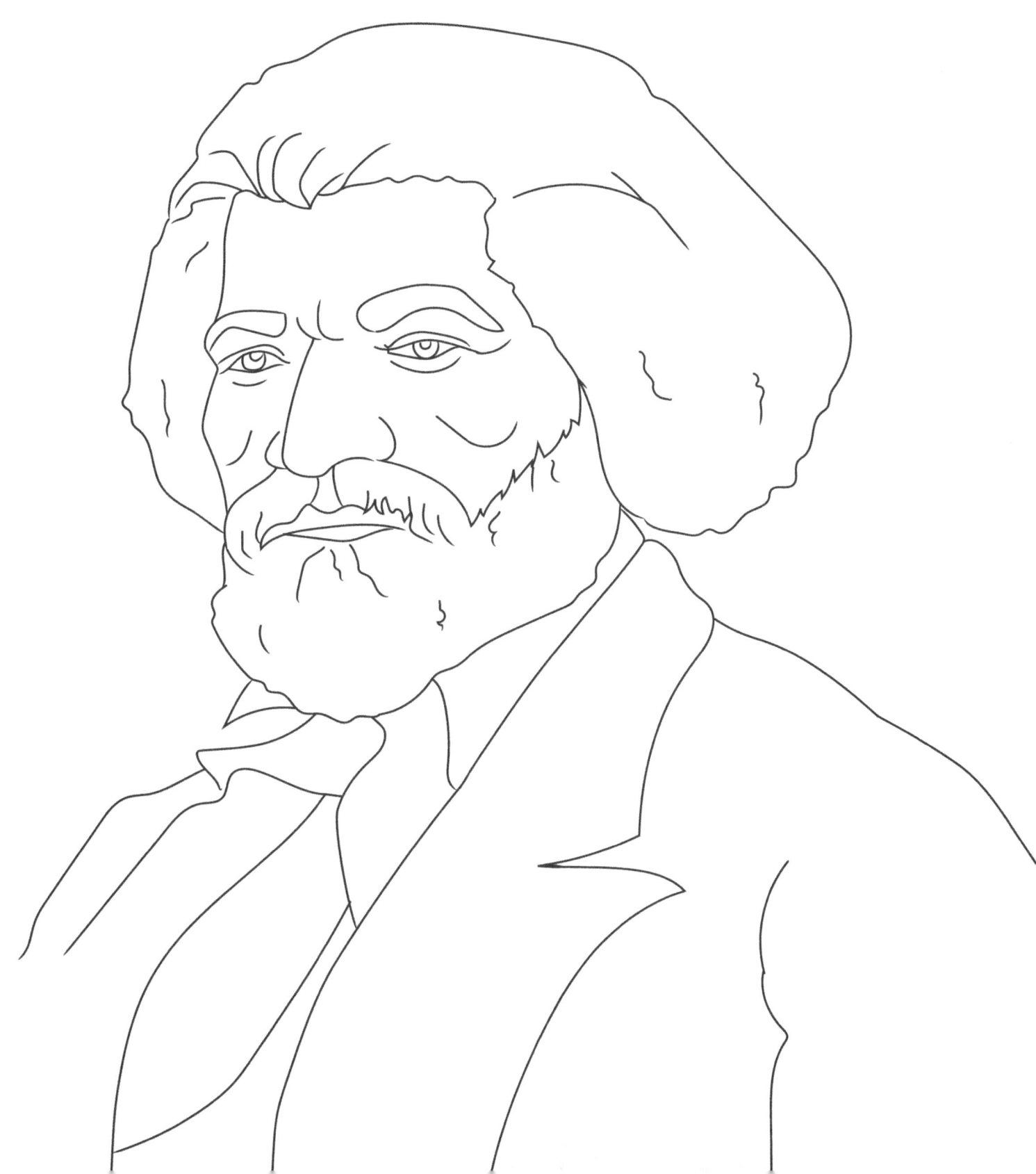

BLACK HISTORY LEGENDS

JACKIE ROBINSON
First African American to play in Major League Baseball.

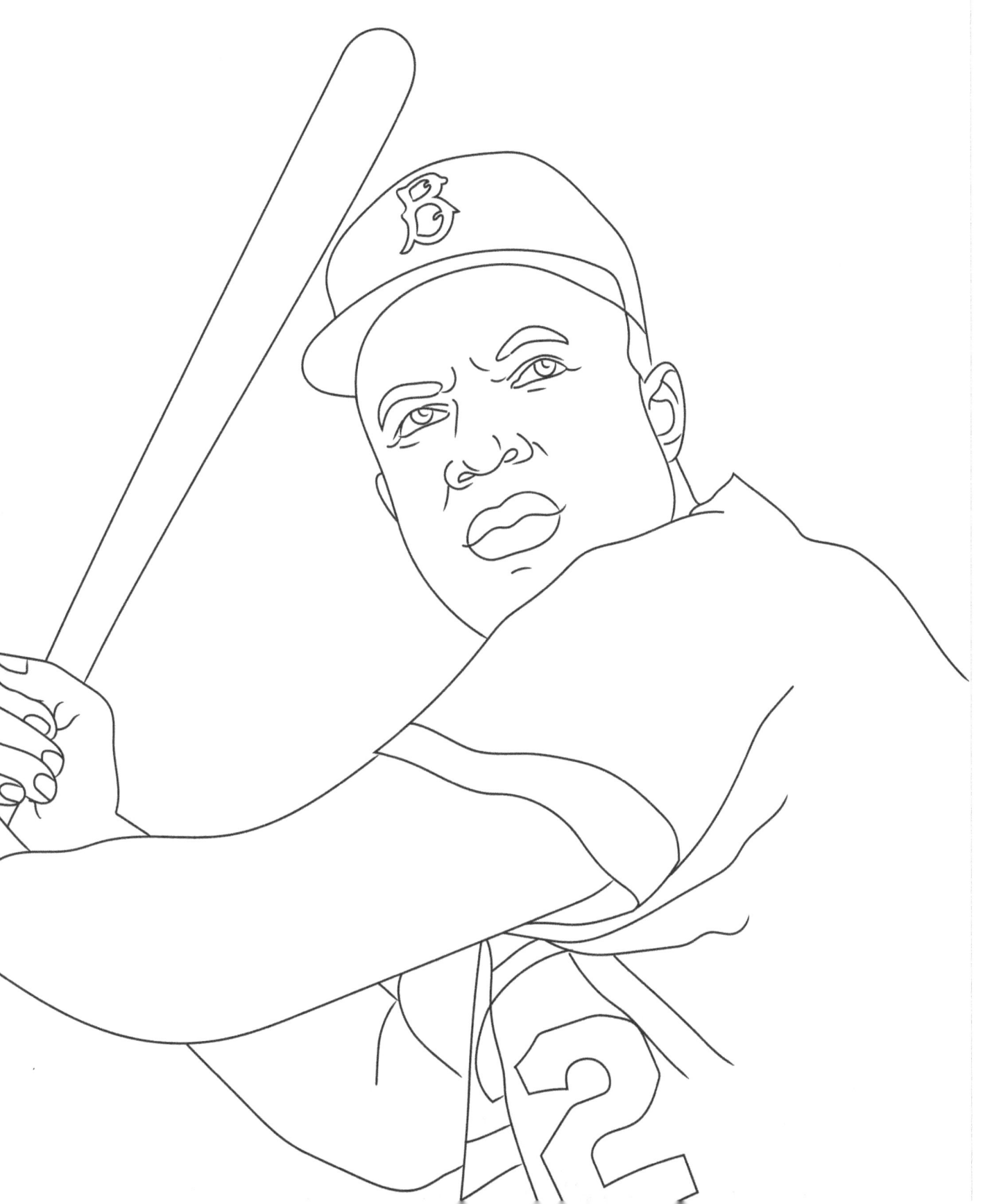

BLACK HISTORY LEGENDS

MAYA ANGELOU
Civil Rights activist and beloved poet.

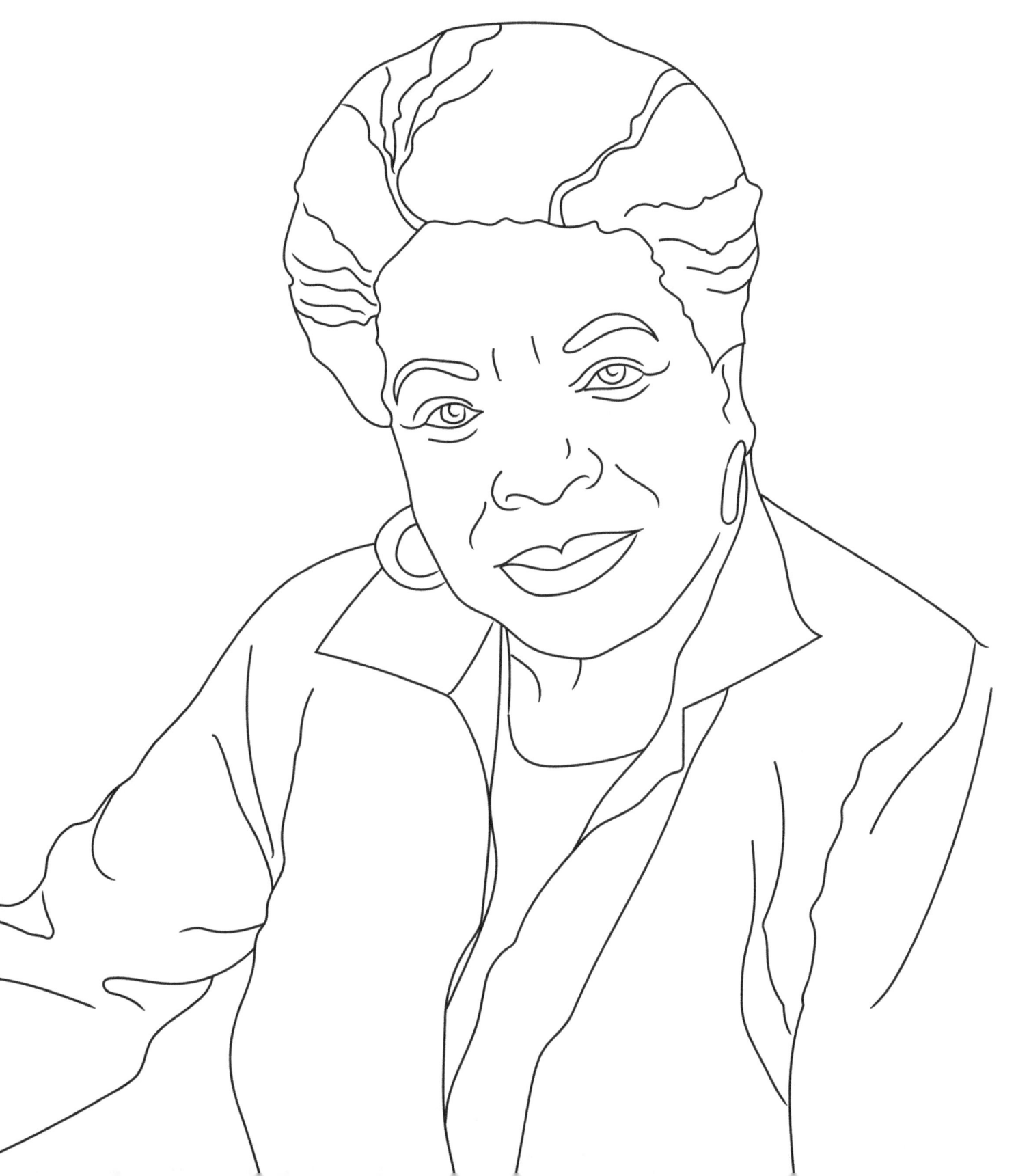

BLACK HISTORY
LEGENDS

MADAM CJ WALKER

Entrepreneur and the wealthiest African American businesswoman of her time.

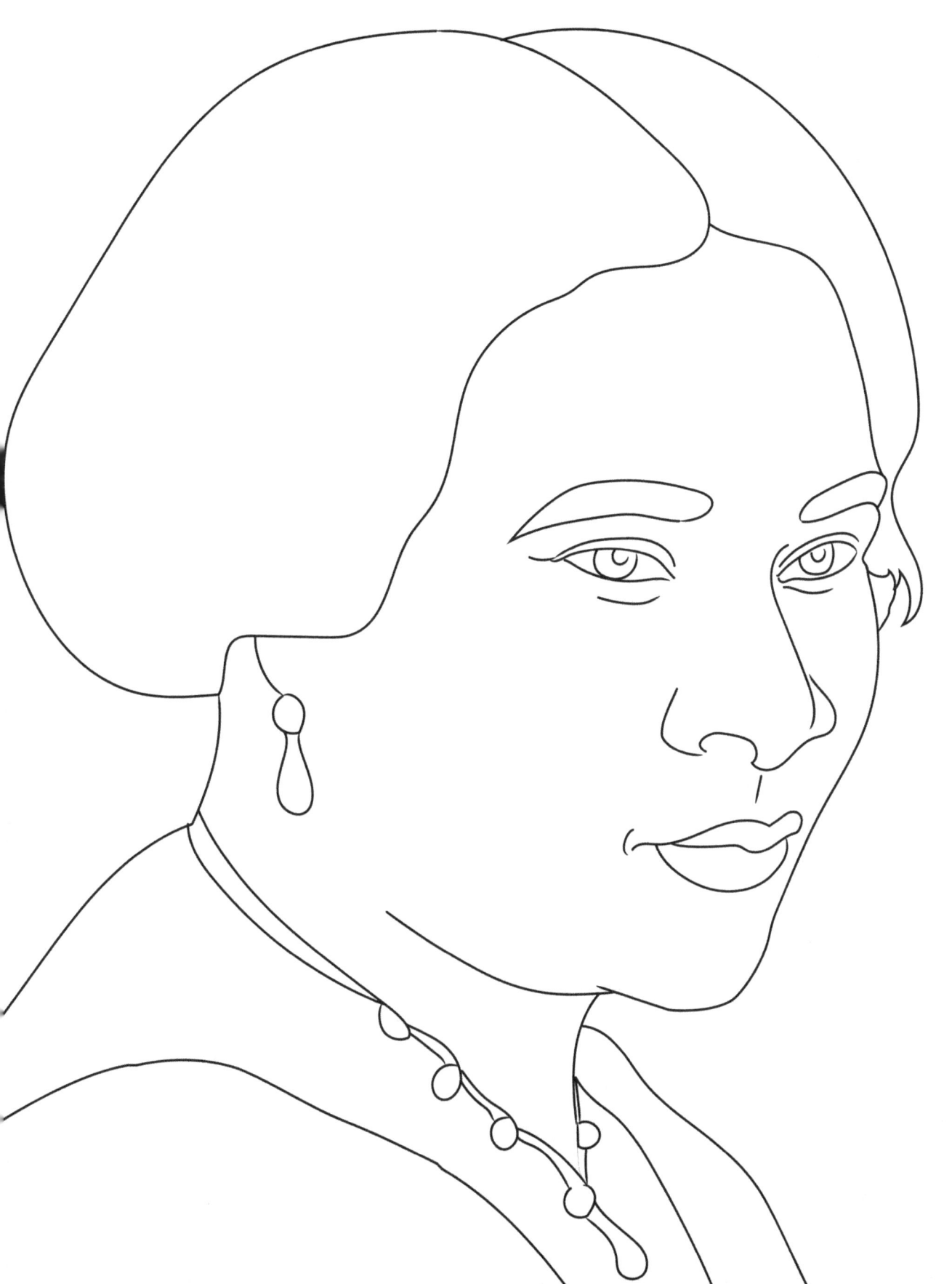

BLACK HISTORY LEGENDS

ROSA PARKS
Civil rights activist who refused to surrender her seat to a white passenger on a segregated bus.

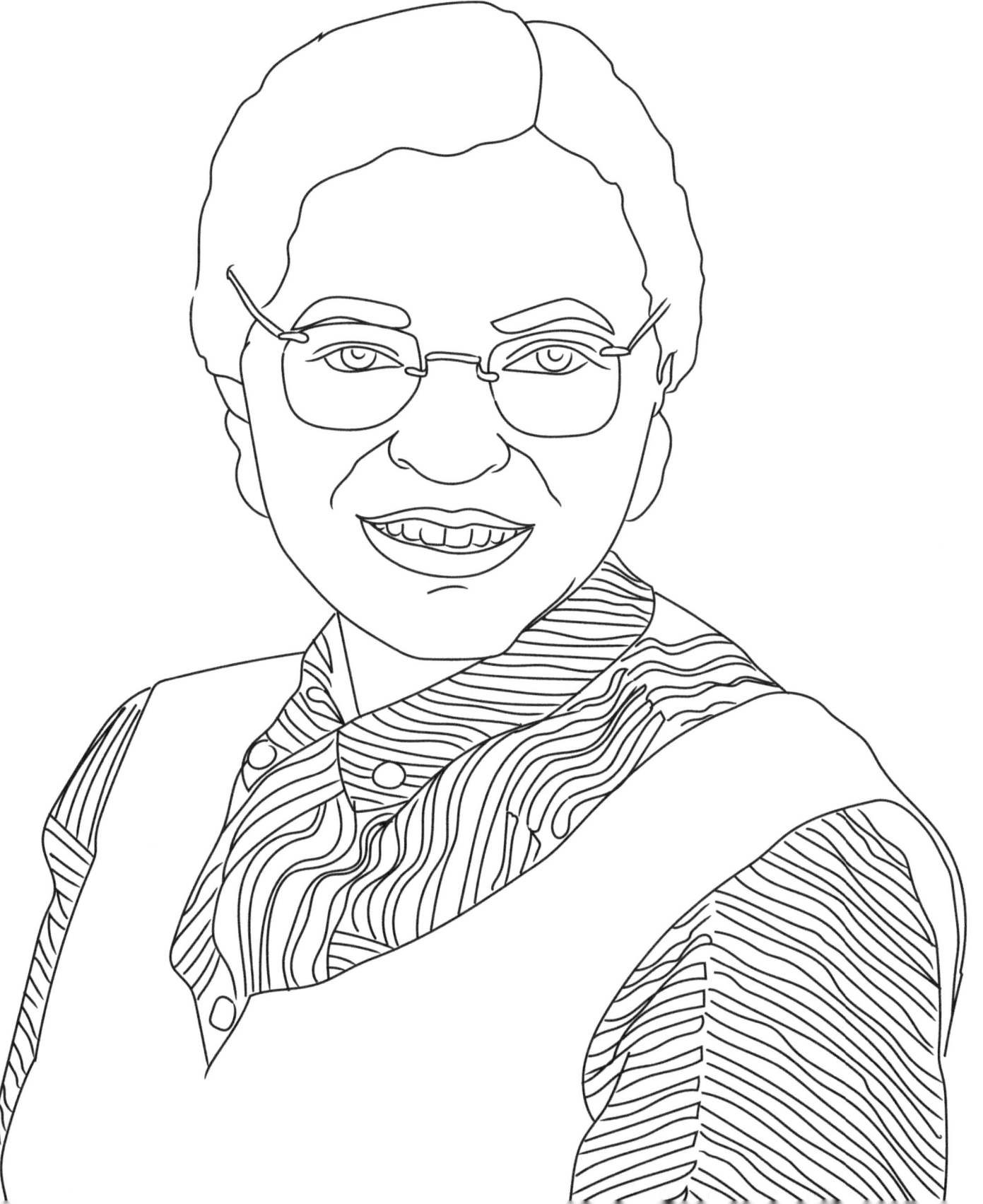

BLACK HISTORY LEGENDS

RONALD McNAIR
NASA astronaut and physicist

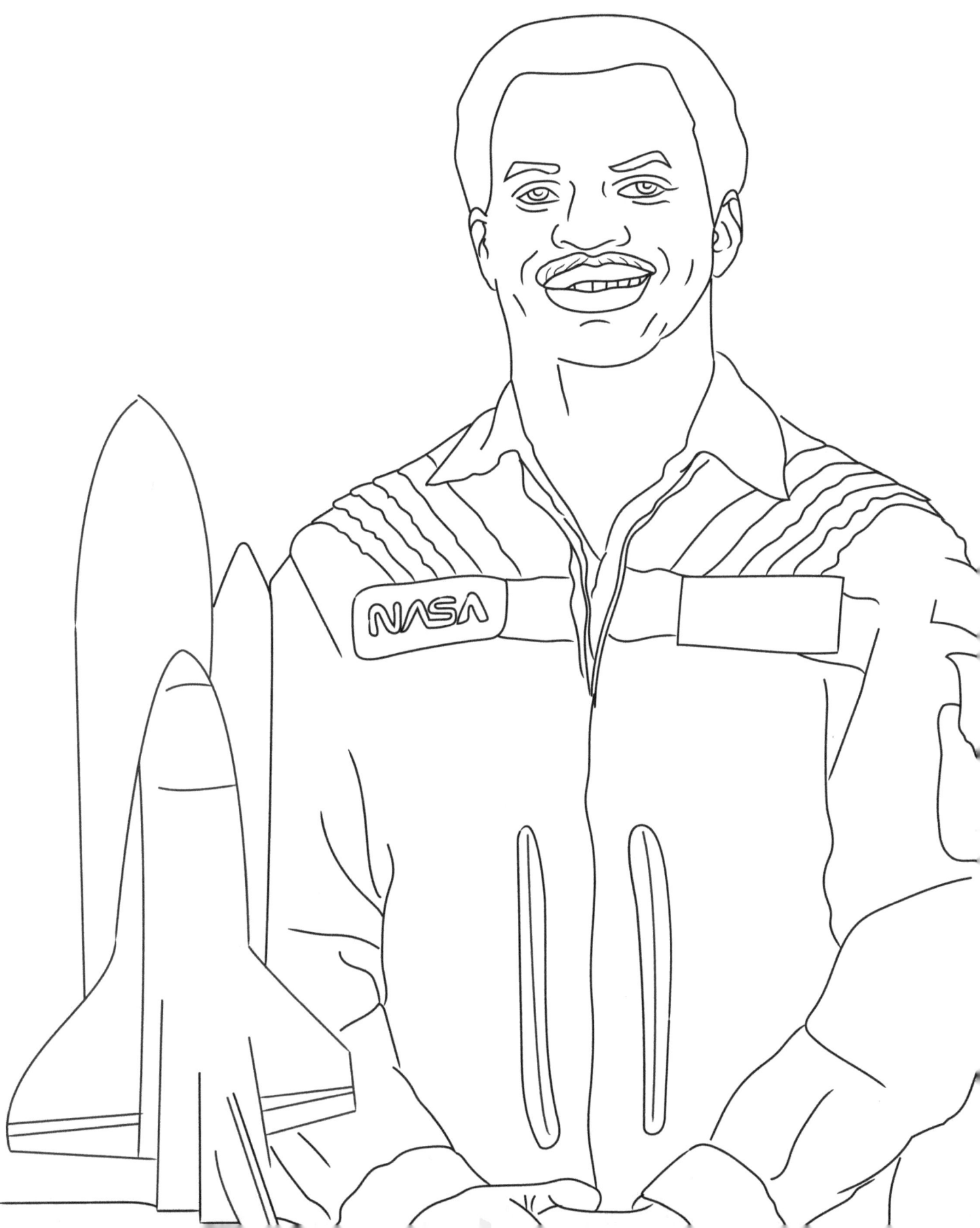

BLACK HISTORY LEGENDS

GEORGE WASHINGTON CARVER

Scientist famous for many inventions and a number of uses for the peanut.

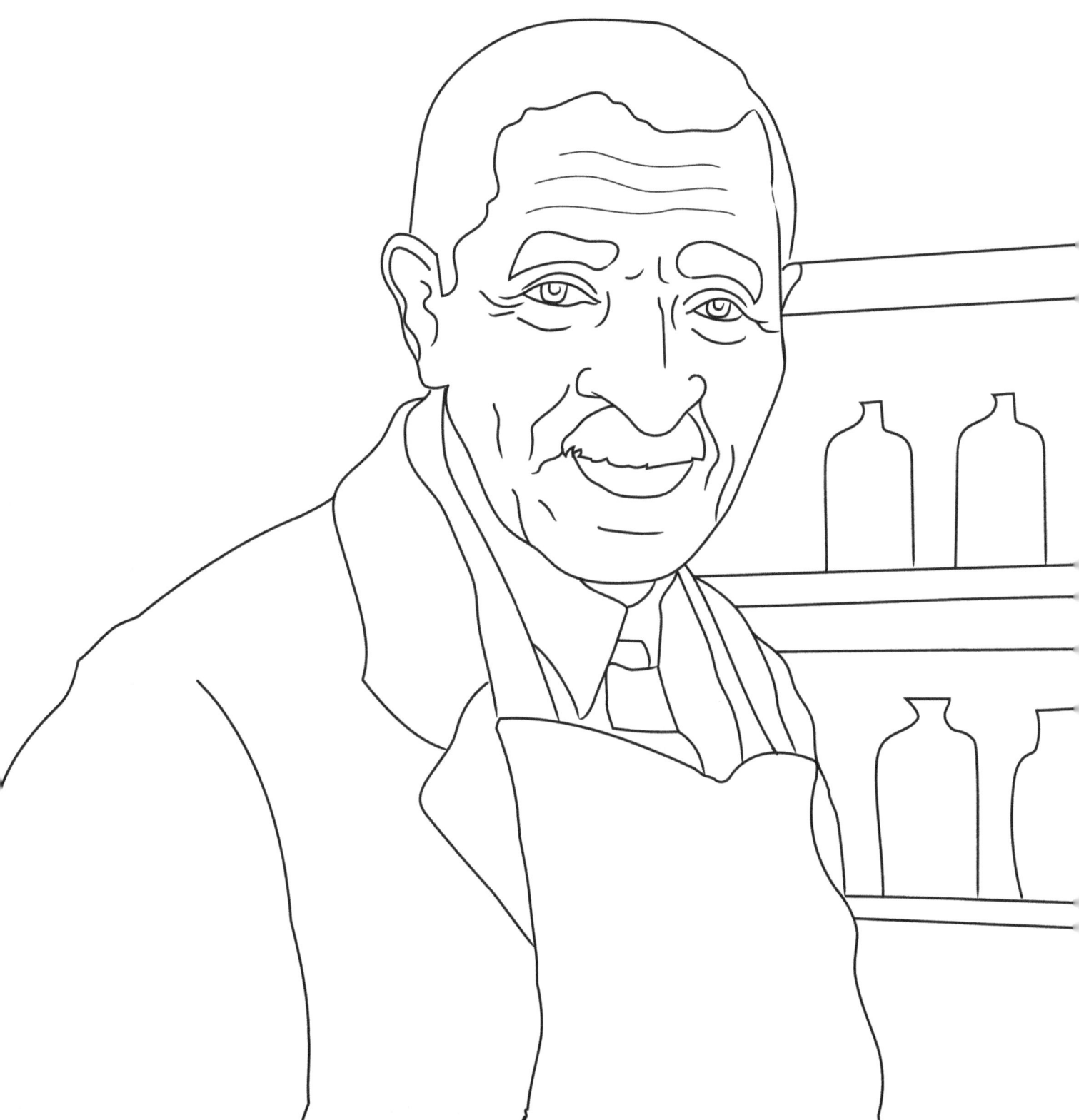

BLACK HISTORY LEGENDS

JESSE OWENS
Made sporting history when he won four gold medals at the 1936 Berlin Olympic Games.

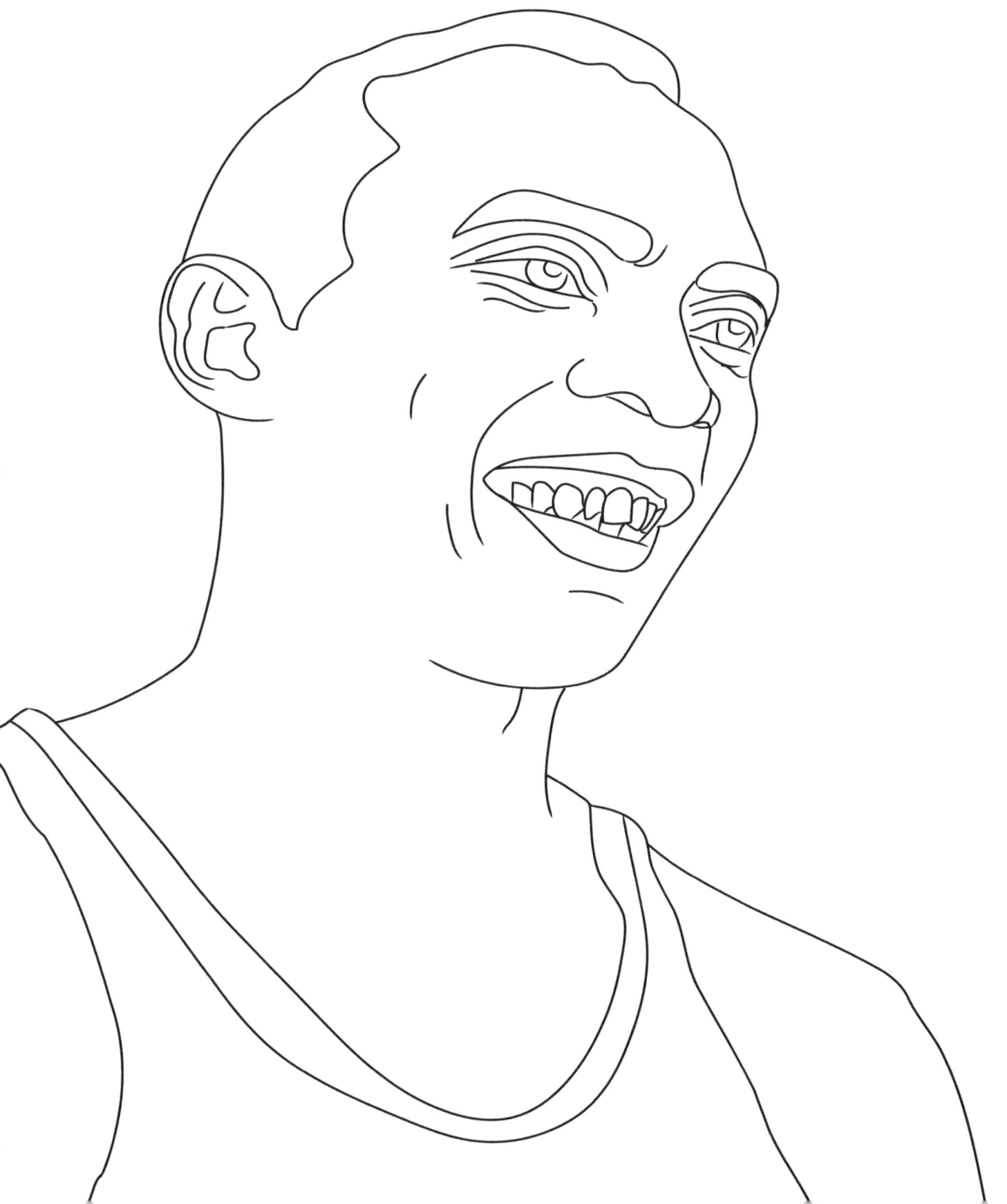

BLACK HISTORY LEGENDS

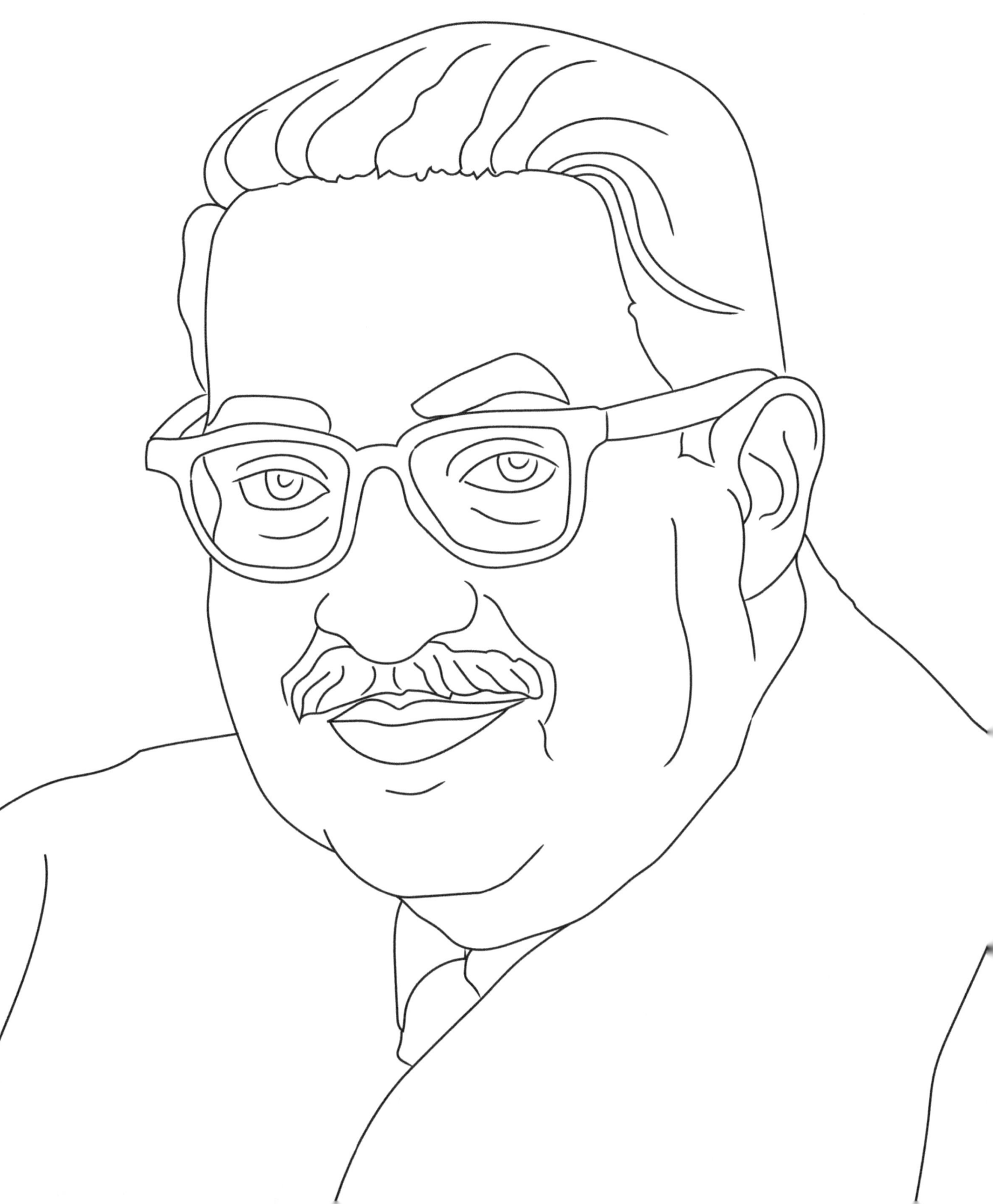

BLACK HISTORY LEGENDS

LANGSTON HUGHES
One of the most prolific writers during the Harlem Renaissance.

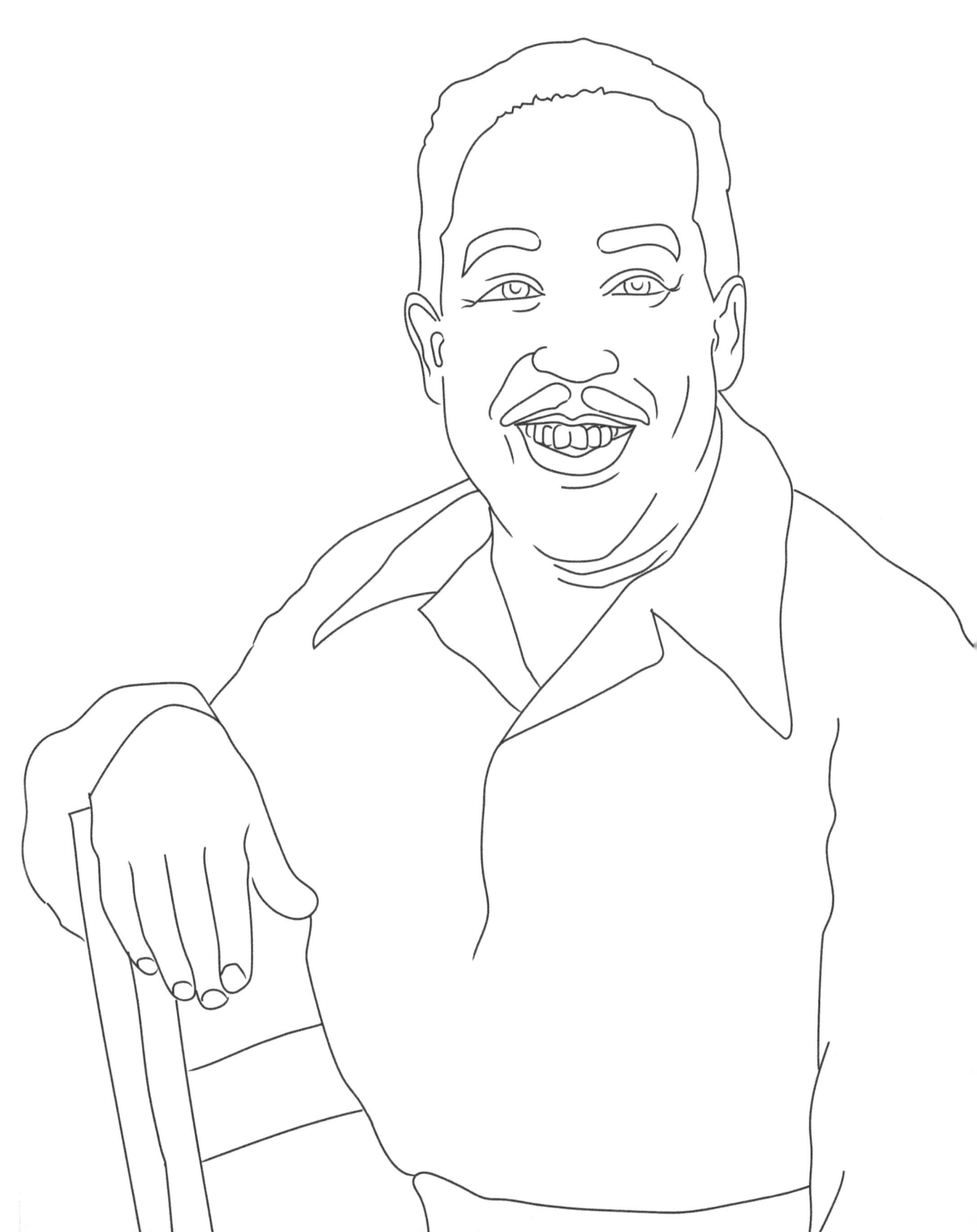

BLACK HISTORY LEGENDS

W.E.B. DU BOIS

Influential Civil Rights activist and Co-Founder of the NAACP.

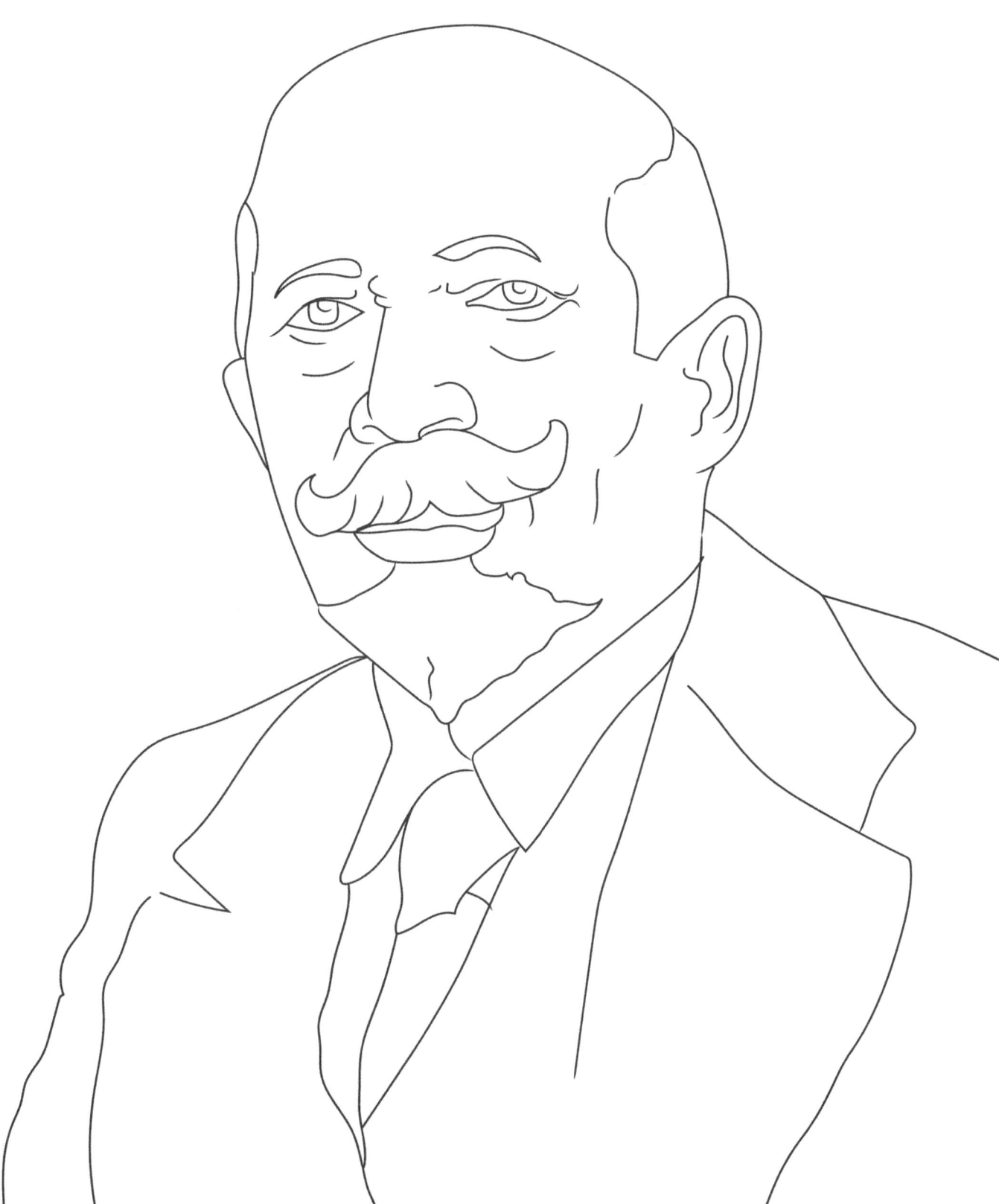

BLACK HISTORY LEGENDS

DORIS MILLER

Manned anti-aircraft guns during the attack on Pearl Harbor and was the first black to be awarded the Navy Cross.

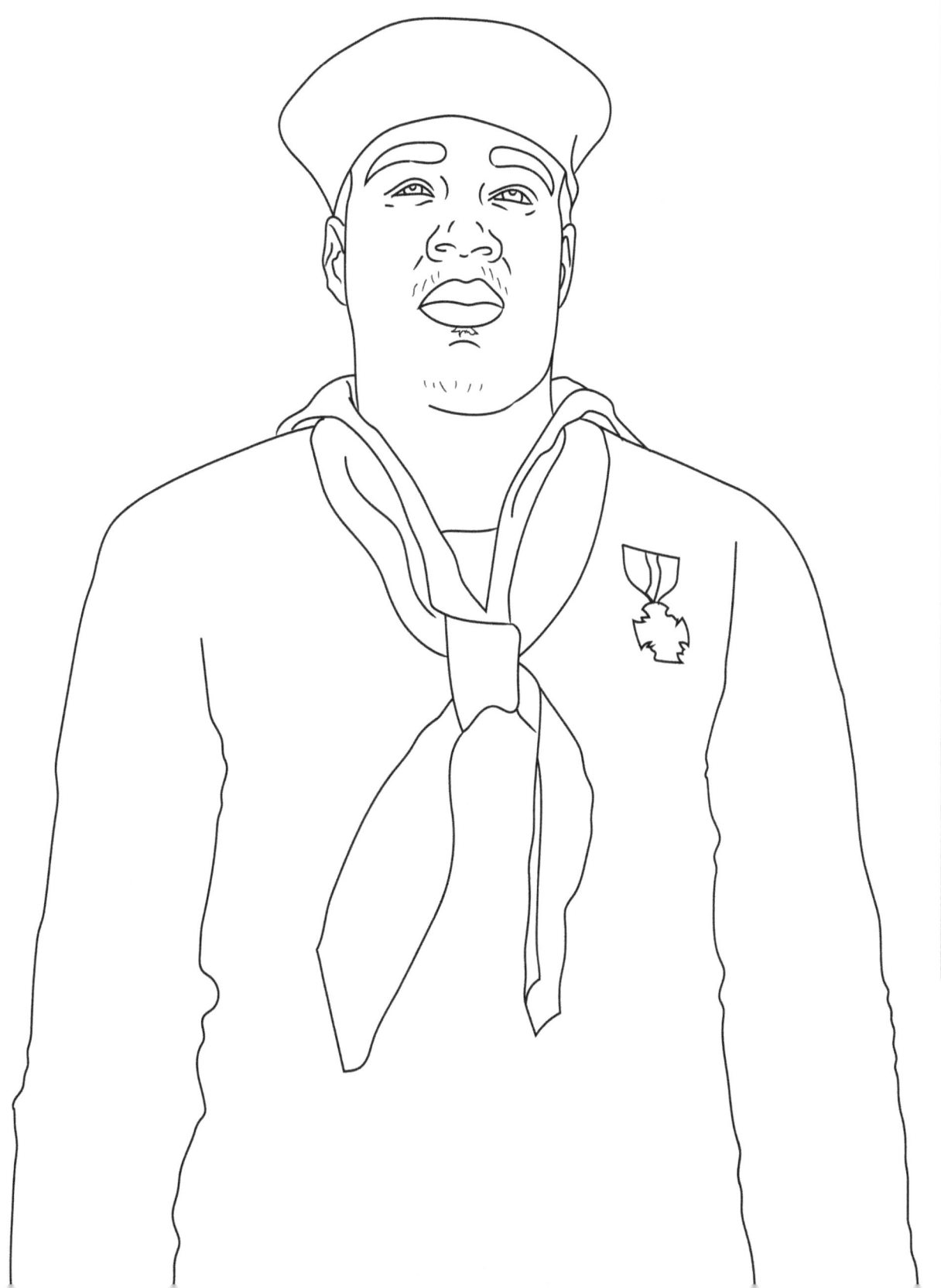

BLACK HISTORY LEGENDS

SHIRLEY CHISHOLM

The first black woman elected to the United States Congress.

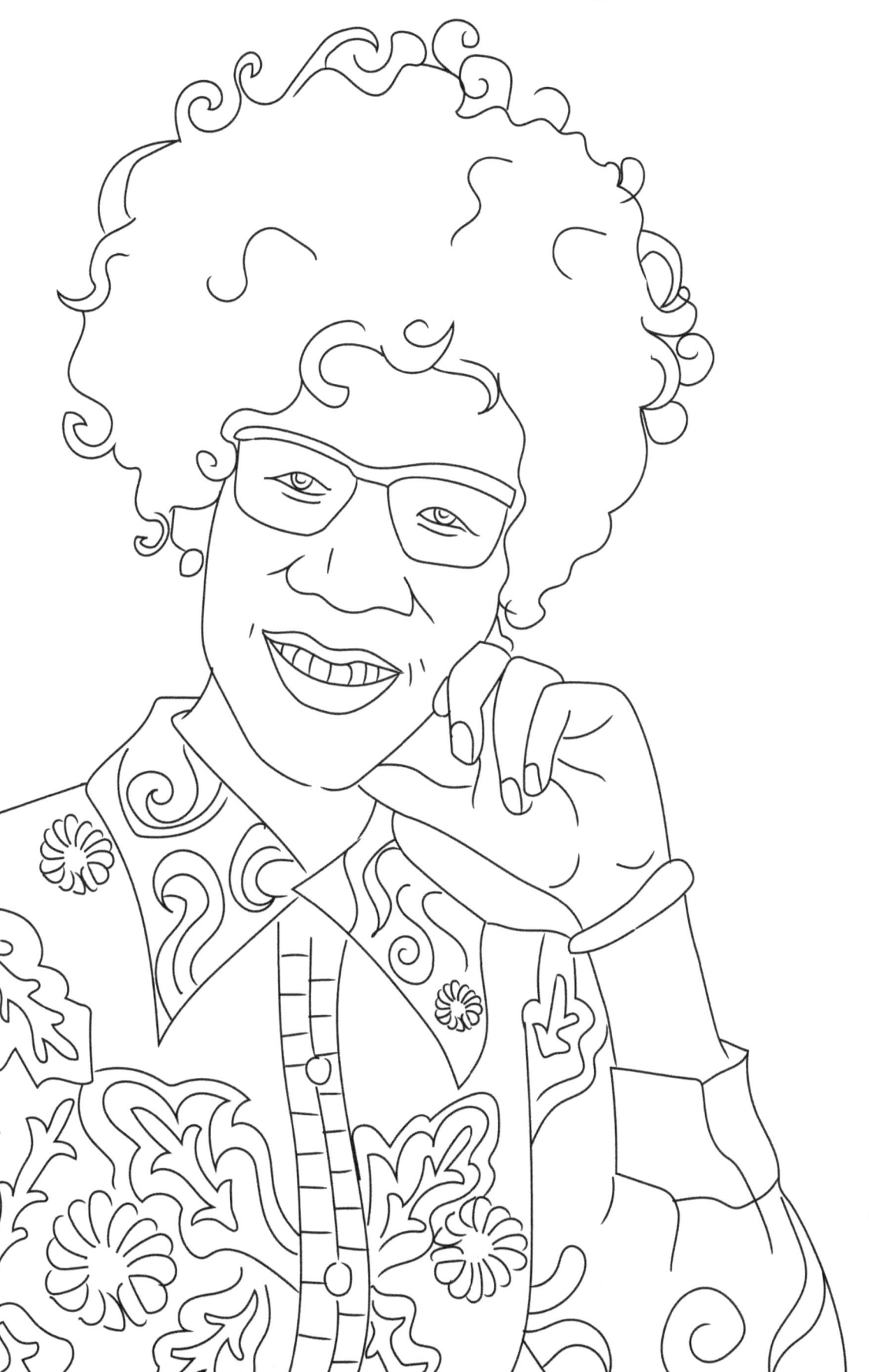

BLACK HISTORY LEGENDS

ZORA NEALE HURSTON
Famed author, anthropologist, and filmmaker.

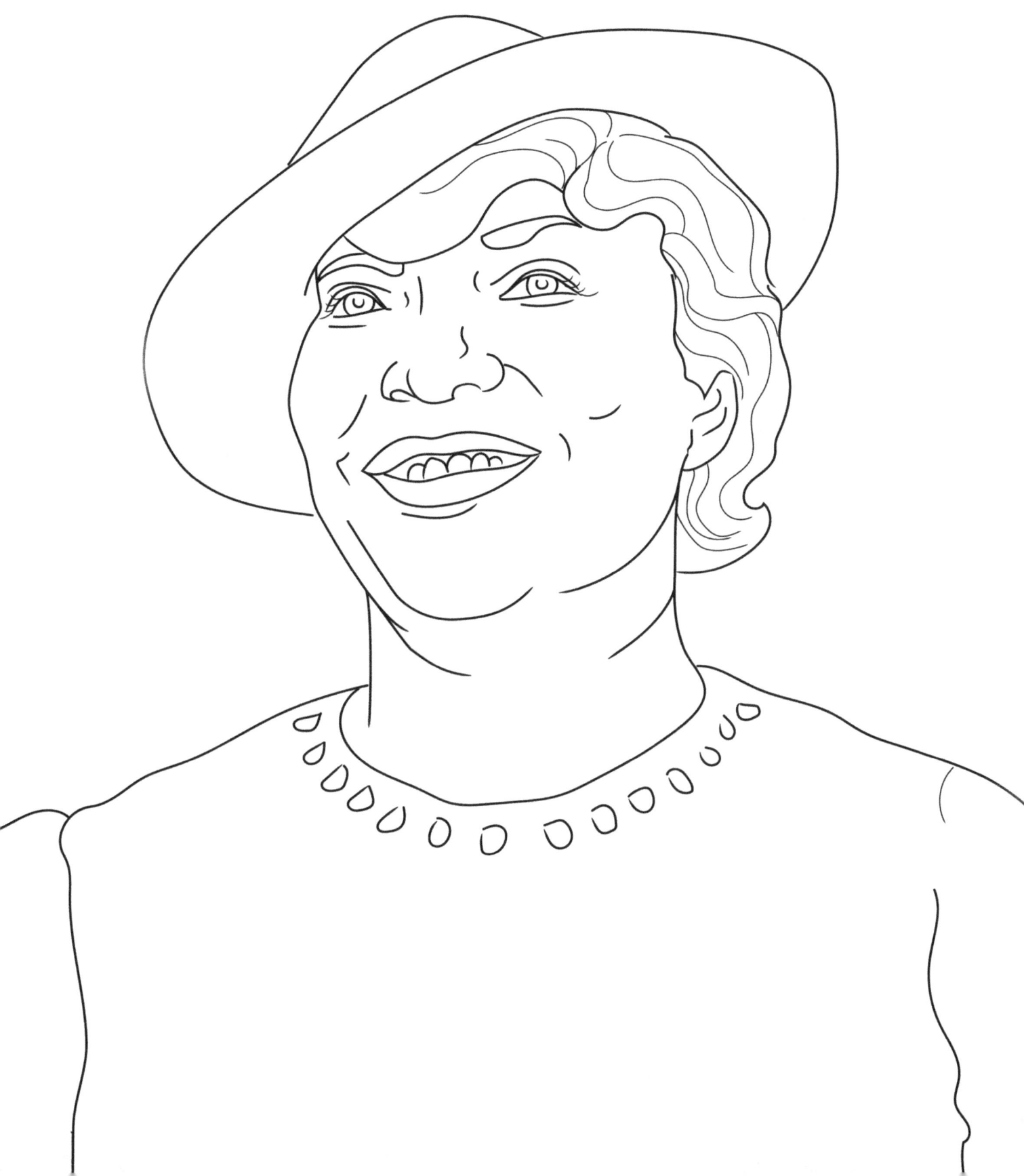

BLACK HISTORY LEGENDS

SOJOURNER TRUTH

Abolitionist and women's rights activist.

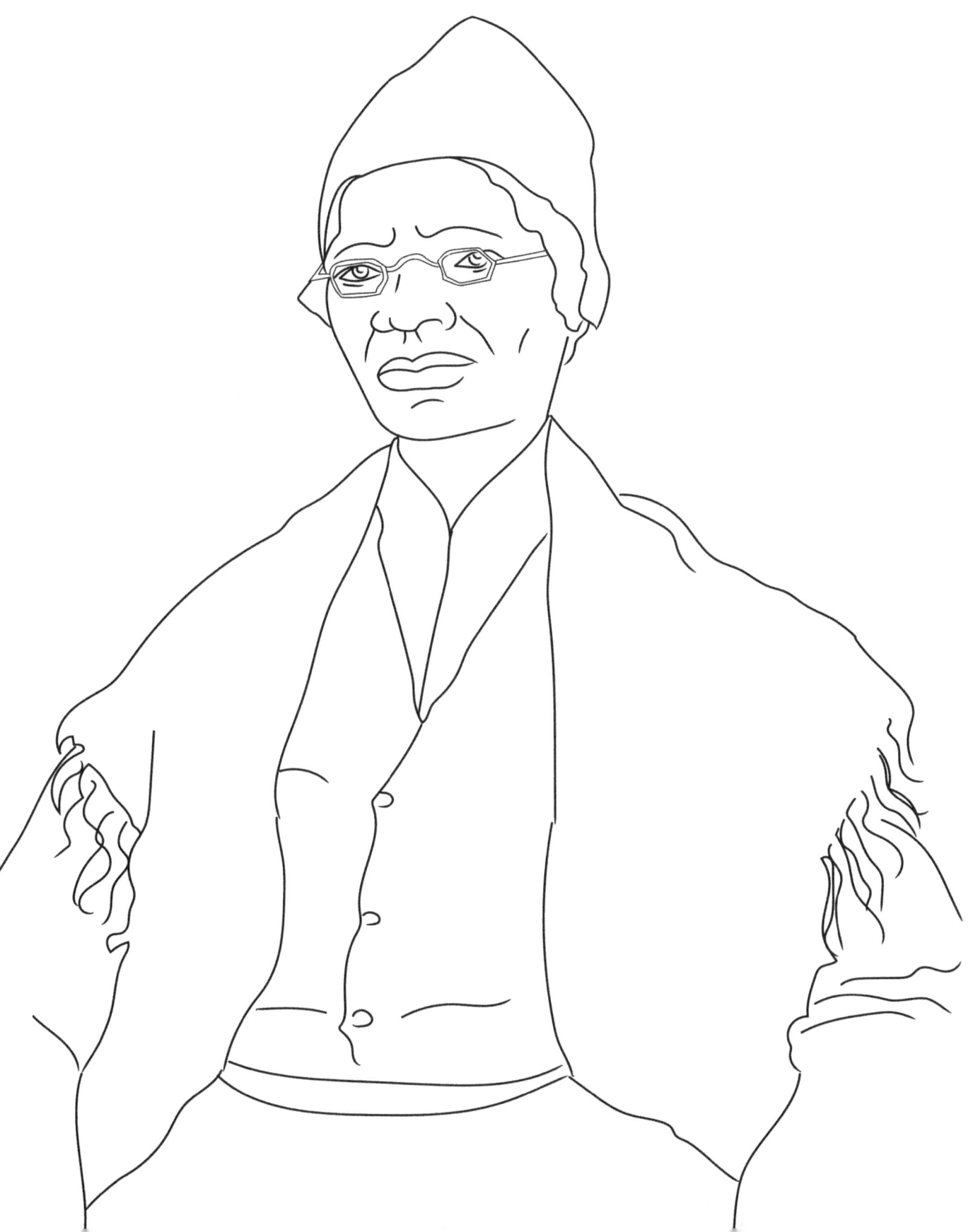

BLACK HISTORY LEGENDS

BOOKER T. WASHINGTON

One of the foremost African American leaders of the late 19th and early 20th and centuries, founding what would later become Tuskegee University.

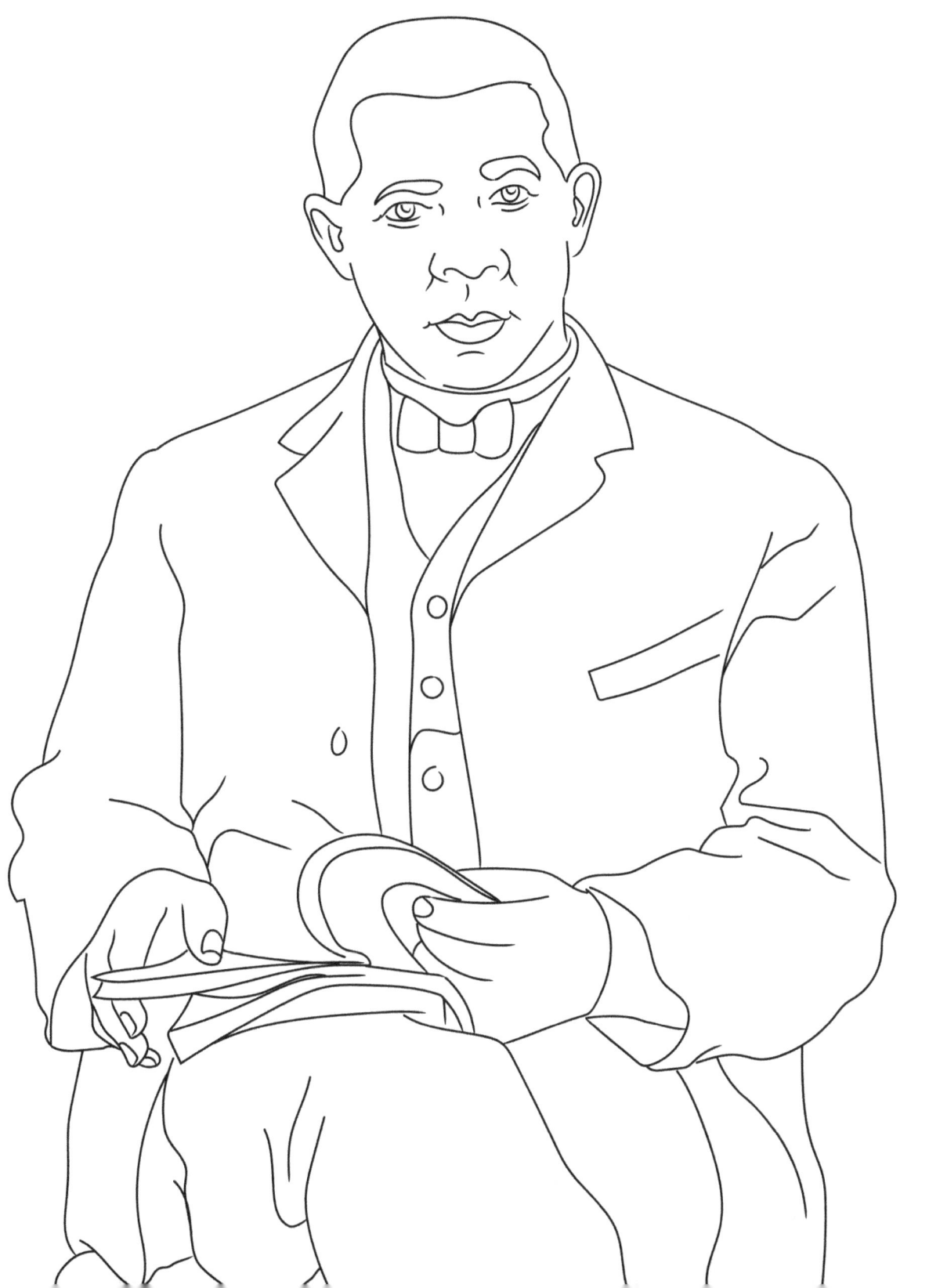

OPRAH WINFREY

Media icon, billionaire, philanthropist and one of the most influential women in the United States.

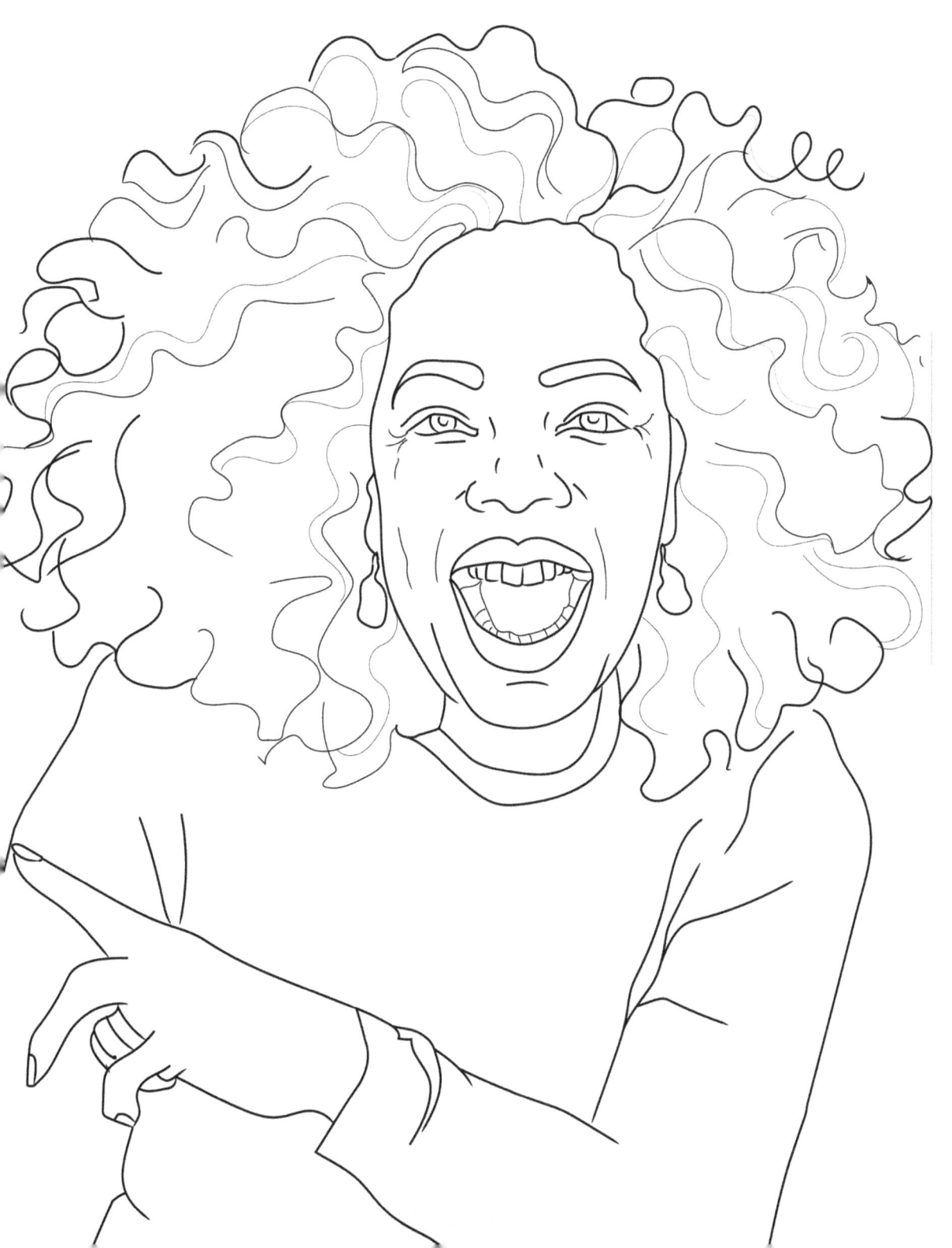

BLACK HISTORY LEGENDS

WILLIE O'REE
First black player in the National Hockey League

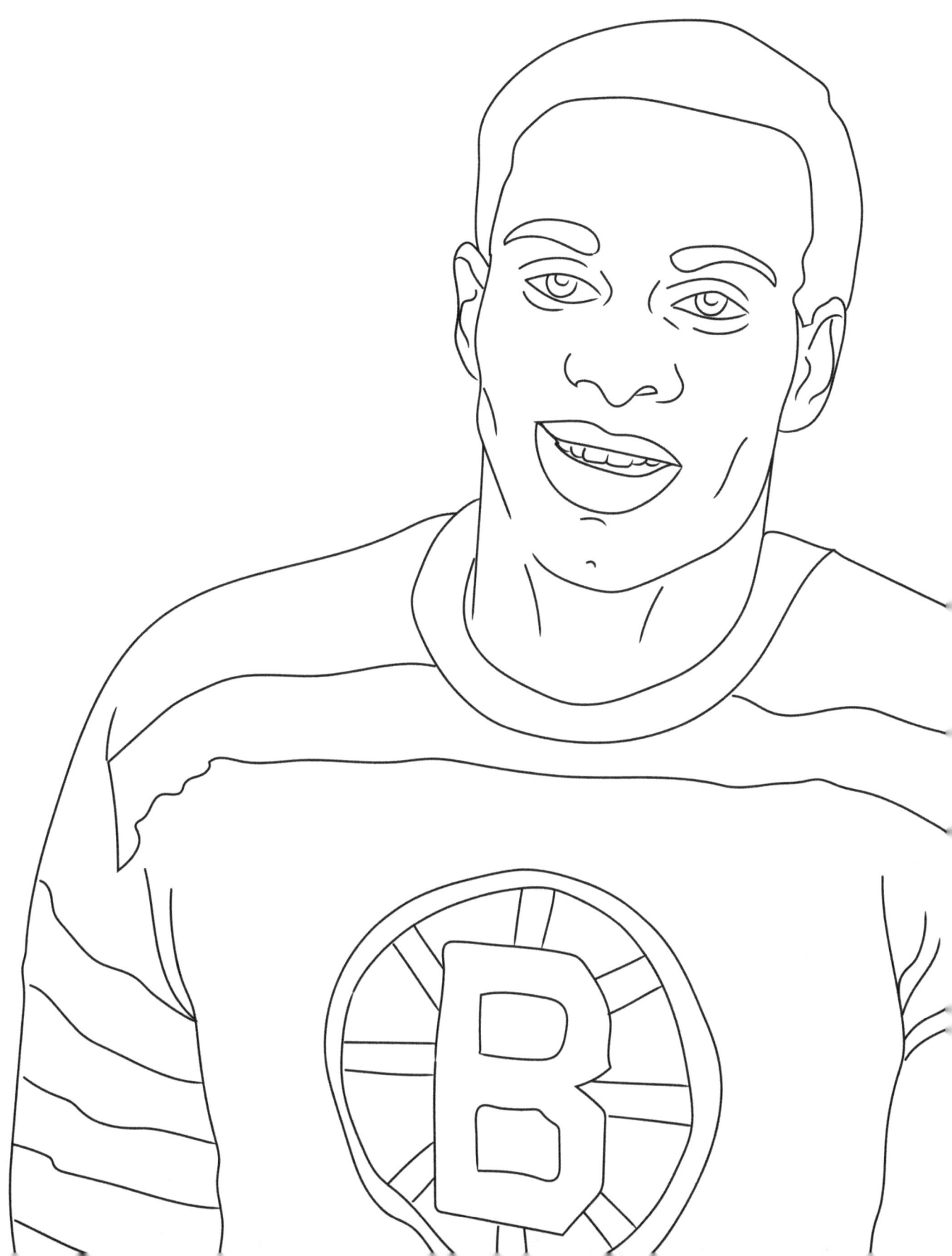

BLACK HISTORY LEGENDS

MATTHEW HENSON

Arctic explorer and likely the first person to reach the geographic North Pole.

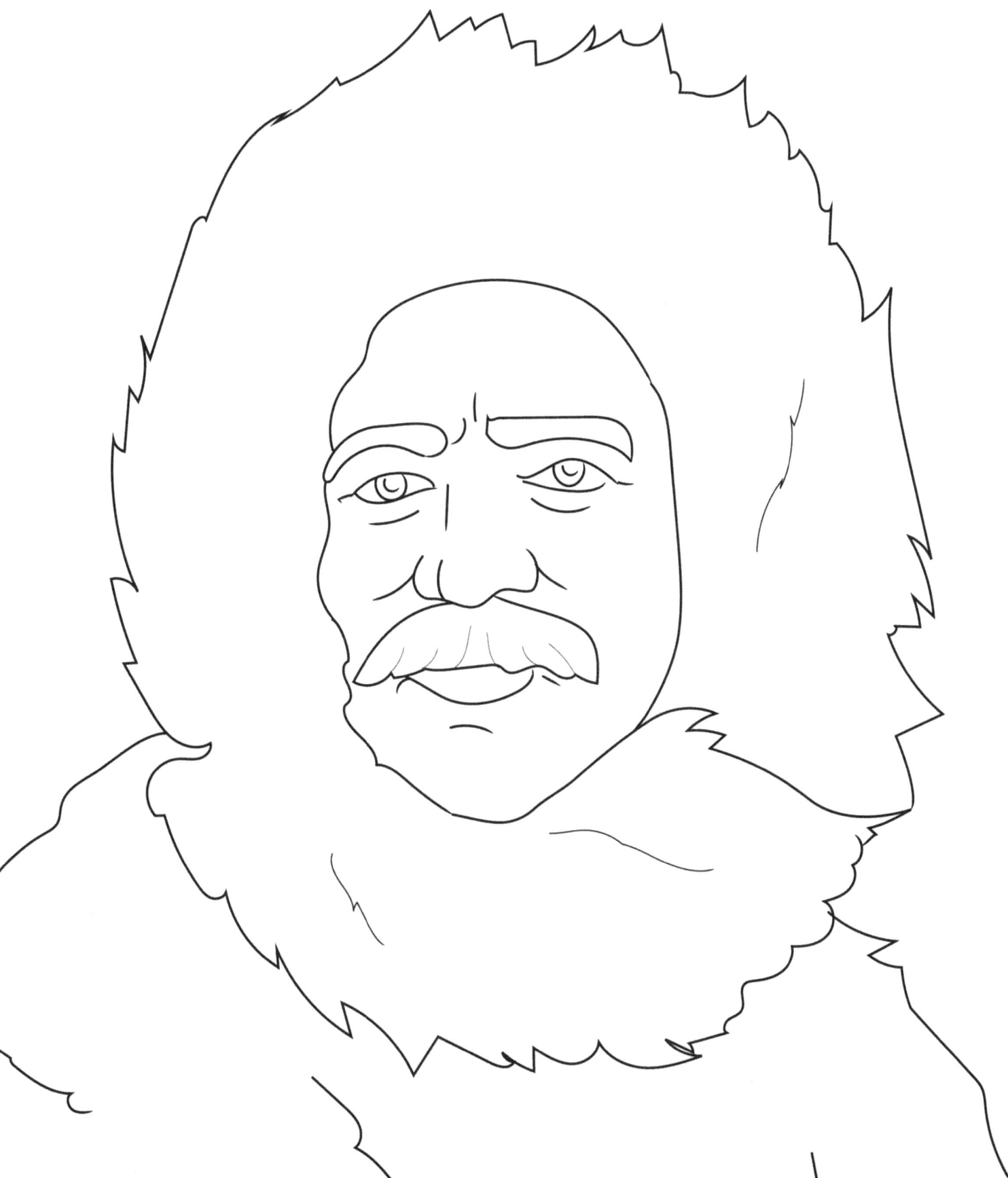

BLACK HISTORY LEGENDS

NELSON MANDELA

South African anti-apartheid revolutionary, political leader, and philanthropist who became President of South Africa.

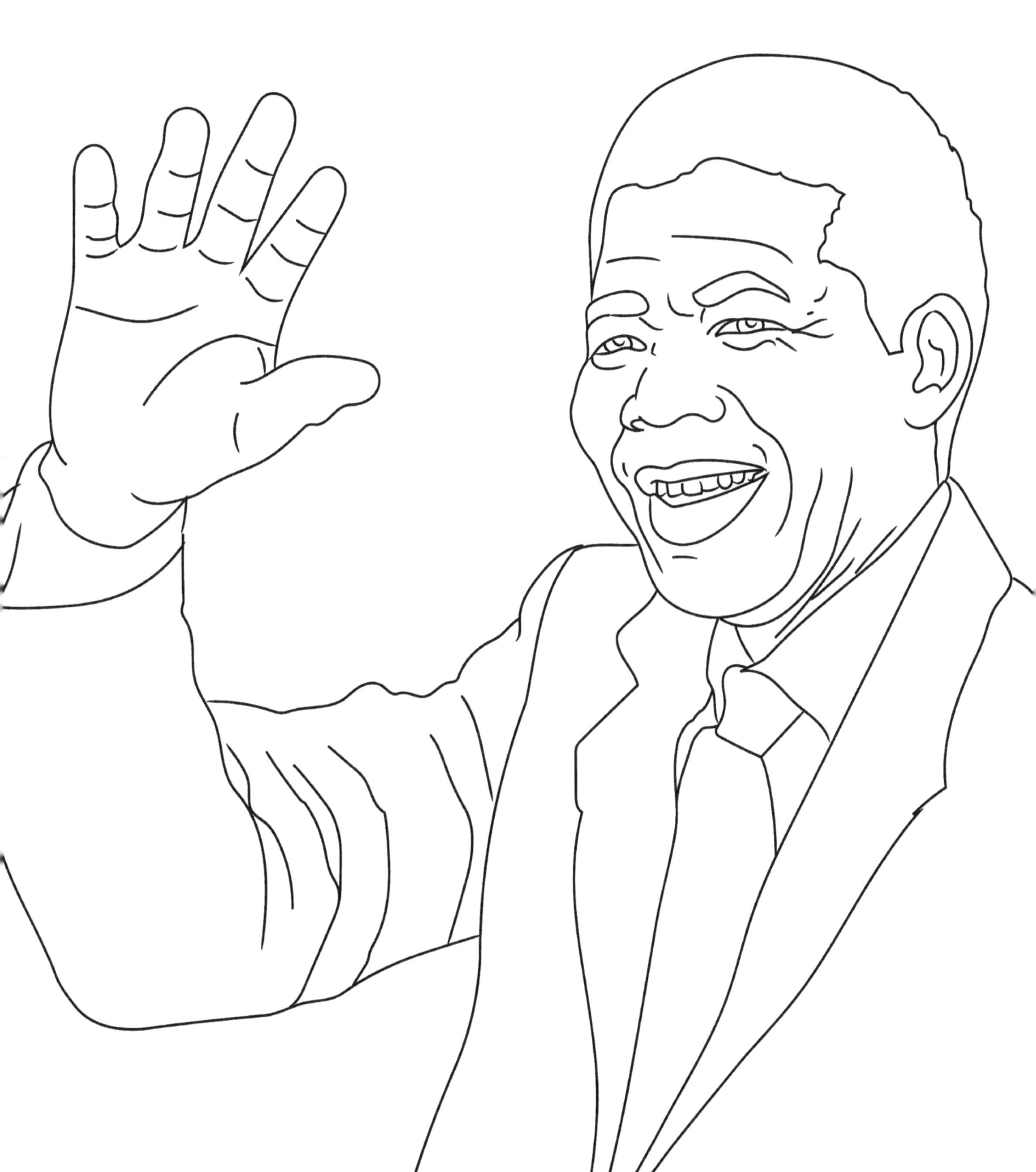

BLACK HISTORY LEGENDS

ELIJAH McCOY

Inventor and Engineer who improved train travel through his works.

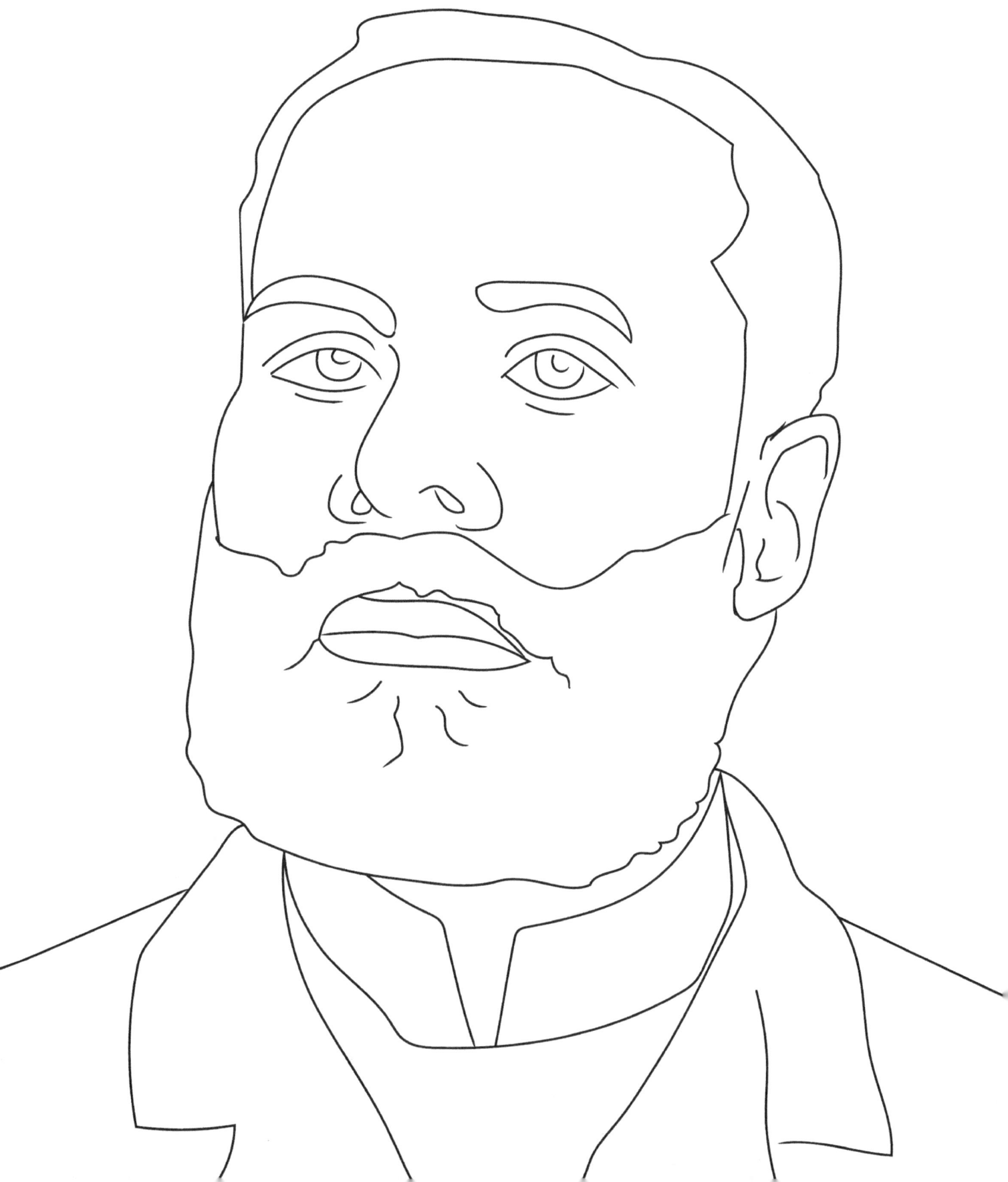

BLACK HISTORY LEGENDS

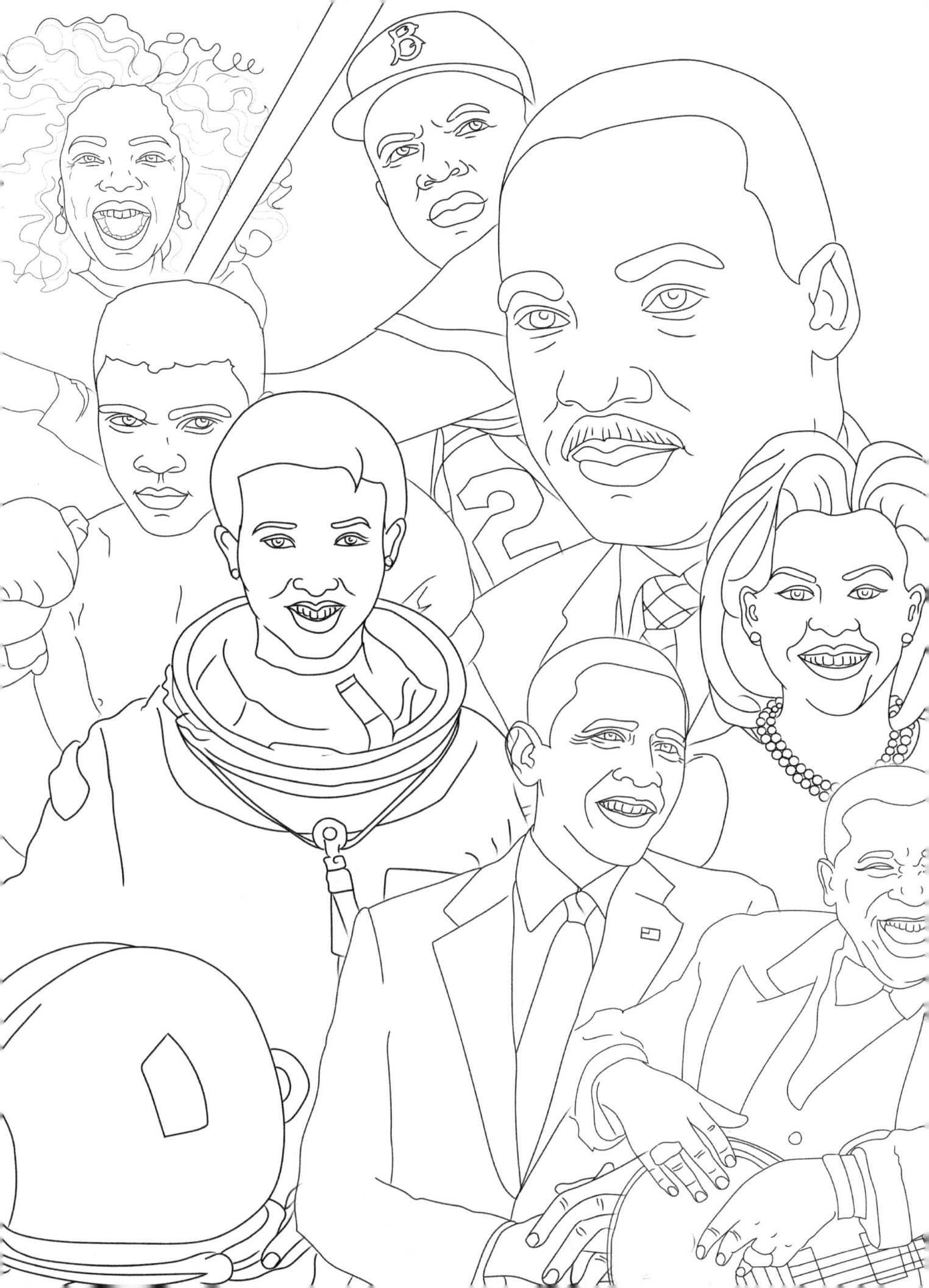

BLACK HISTORY LEGENDS

www.ingramcontent.com/pod-product-compliance
Lightning Source LLC
Chambersburg PA
CBHW060439220526
45465CB00008B/3203